VOICES OF THE SOUL

ANSWERED IN

GOD.

BY

REV. JOHN REID.

NEW YORK:
ROBERT CARTER & BROTHERS,
530 BROADWAY.

1866.

Stereotyped by SMITH & McDOUGAL, 82 & 84 Beekman Street.

NOTE.

THE manuscript of the present work was read by Tayler Lewis, LL.D., and by William G. T. Shedd, D.D. Their views in regard to it are expressed in the following statements:—

Prof. Lewis says: "I am glad that I retained your manuscript until I had read the second half. My interest in the work increased at every page, and I can sincerely express to you my opinion that it has a substantial value, both of thought and style, that ought to commend it to all thoughtful readers. The charm of your book to me is its continuous flow of most serious and impressive thoughts. I would not hesitate to compare the last chapter with anything I have read from Bushnell or Isaac Taylor; thoughts of the highest order are expressed in a fitting style of language. Your work cannot fail to be popular in the best sense ot the word, because it so reveals each reader's mind to himself."

Professor Shedd thus writes: "I return your manuscript to-day by express, and am much obliged to you for the opportunity of perusing it. It is a work of originality and power. This is the impression which it has made upon me, and made with energy. I have rarely perused a treatise which has issued so evidently as this has from prolonged searching reflection, and strong earnest conviction. You have discussed the serious themes of evangelical religion in a manner that invests them with fresh interest for the believer and also for the unbeliever. For your method is psychological. The appeal to consciousness is direct, continual, and penetrating; so that both the natural and spiritual man will be interested, each in his own way. No educated person, be he Christian or skeptic, will fail to read your book through, if he begins it. Without committing myself to every particular in the work, it is my belief that it will prove to be a valuable addition to our religious literature."

PREFACE TO THE THIRD EDITION.

WITH the exception of a change in a few words, the third edition is the same as the first. A hint respecting the plan of the work, we simply offer in this place.

The soul needs a way to reach God; a way to become holy, a way to become happy. Hence the book is divided into three parts; and it is shown how the wants of the mind can be met in a Redeemer, Restorer and Satisfier. *Mediation* must come first, then *restoration*, then *satisfaction*. This is the order of nature, and this we have followed. The treatise is to be taken as a whole, and is to be read from the beginning to the end, in order to receive the impression that is aimed at. Although the immediate aim is to connect the soul and God together, yet every one can see that that revolves itself into another thought, viz., that the doctrine of the book being true, the Christian religion is the only hope of man. By that he finds a complete ransom, a complete cure, and a complete blessedness. The work, therefore, is really an indirect argument for the truth of Christianity.

I may be asked whether the VOICES OF THE SOUL be those of simple nature, or nature as touched by that which is Divine? To answer this, in every case, is not easy. To what extent redemptive agencies affect the souls of the entire race, no one can tell. It may be that broken and bent rays from a higher world glimmer in the darkest human spirit that is to be found upon this earth. An *abstract, natural man* may not exist; one whose development is carried forward outside of any influence from Calvary may not be found. However this may be, the men where Christianity is known are manifestly moved by it to a greater or less extent. What I would say, then, is this: the *rudiments* of the VOICES OF THE SOUL are found in all; but their strength and peculiar form are the result of redemptive forces. Apart from any change of heart, and before any change of heart, there is a work performed by Divine truth and the Divine Spirit. God leads men to cry and lament, and then he places before them the remedy they need.

PREFACE.

THERE are two words that are much used at present—the words infinite and finite. These may be said to characterize modern thinking. The people as yet are content with the words God and man. They sometimes, however, speak of the human and the divine, or the natural and the supernatural, catching these words from a class of minds that are wont to fence with them. It is evident that we are in the midst of a great discussion,—a discussion that touches upon the highest and holiest themes of existence. Whether we have a Christian redemption and a Christian God are the points that are to be settled. No good man need be afraid that the religion in which he has trusted is about to slip away from beneath him, as if it were like some island of the deep that had been carefully surveyed and its exact place set down in the chart, while all at once it sinks to rise not again. We have no fears respecting the fate of Christianity. Almost are we thankful for the assaults that are made upon it, as these tend but to make manifest its divine durability. The fiercer the attack, the more complete and successful the repulse.

Calm, considerate thinking is just now much needed. Many are earnest, warlike, but not sufficiently awed and controlled by the tremendous issues of life. A deeper insight into human nature and a more profound conception of the Godhead are the wants of the time. As it respects the ultimate bearing of the present treatise, that will be perceived by an attentive perusal of it. The soul is taken as it is, and the attempt is made to find that in God which will meet and match it.

CONTENTS.

PART I.

VOICES OF THE SOUL ANSWERED IN GOD THE REDEEMER.

CHAPTER I.

AN INCARNATION OF GOD A WANT OF MIND.

CHAPTER II.

DEEP CONVICTION OF SIN: NEED OF A DIVINE SAVIOUR.

CHAPTER III.

CONSCIOUSNESS OF GUILT: NEED OF DIVINE ATONEMENT.

SECTION I.

THE WORKING OF GUILT.

SECTION II.

A DIVINE ATONEMENT NEEDED TO MEET THE CLAIMS OF GUILT.

CHAPTER IV.

LAW BROKEN: THE DIVINE SUSTAINER OF LAW.

SECTION I.

MAN A TRANSGRESSOR OF LAW.

CHAPTER VI.

HUMAN SORROW: THE DIVINE SYMPATHIZER.

SECTION I.

THE VOICE OF SORROW.

SECTION II.

THE GOD-MAN A SYMPATHIZER.

PART II.

VOICES OF THE SOUL ANSWERED IN GOD THE RESTORER.

CHAPTER I.

VESTIGES OF THE DIVINE IN MAN NOT SUFFICIENT TO DEVELOP HOLINESS APART FROM THE SUPERNATURAL.

CHAPTER IV.

THE SOUL IN RUINS: A SUPERNATURAL RESTORATION REQUIRED.

CHAPTER V.

NEED OF REDEMPTION: THE SUPERNATURAL REMEDY FOUND.

CHAPTER VI.

MAN ESTRANGED FROM GOD: THE PHILOSOPHY OF THE SUPERNATURAL CURE.

PART III.

VOICES OF THE SOUL ANSWERED IN GOD THE SATISFIER.

CHAPTER I.

HINTS RESPECTING A NEBULOUS REGION IN THE SOUL, AND ITS RELATION TO THE FUTURE DEVELOPMENTS OF GOD.

CHAPTER II.

THE FINITE DISSATISFIED WITH LESS THAN THE INFINITE.

CHAPTER III.

THE SOUL A PRAYER WHOSE ANSWER IS GOD.

CHAPTER IV.

GOD THE HOME OF THE SOUL.

PART I.

Voices of the Soul answered in God the Redeemer.

CHAPTER I.

AN INCARNATION OF GOD A WANT OF MIND.

I do not know but that it is the usual fate of mortals to pass through the most momentous periods of history without any due realization of the magnitude of the scene that is about them, or any correct conception of a future that is always more or less clearly foreshadowed by a present, even as the sun paints and illumines the eastern sky while as yet he is beneath the horizon. The disciples slept while Jesus was in an agony for a fallen race, —a type of all the races of men standing unconsciously in the presence of mighty events and an infinite God. There are divine doctrines that equally fail to awaken interest and emotion corresponding to their nature. The incarnation of God is one of these. No human soul is all intent to witness those great movements of the Deity, which, like waves of love, roll onward to bless mankind. There is a lethargy of soul touching the whole sphere of divine realities. This lethargy in many cases seems to have taken form, as if it had become a dark prison of unbelief, in the midst of which the human spirit is attempting to live without the eternal Light, and the friendly visitations of eternal Goodness.

It will not do to say that an incarnation of God is impossible. That point cannot be proved. If God can create, he also can become incarnate. Creation shows that the Timeless has entered into time, that the Infinite has connected himself with the finite. If he can thus act, why may he not also assume human nature? That there is mystery here is admitted. Creation is a mystery; the incarnation of a divine person is a mystery. It makes no difference whether we trace back matter to the time when it may have been a fiery cloud covering space, as if it were a curtain to the tabernacle of God. Go back as we may, creation had a beginning. Science and Scripture make that certain. How God could *begin* to create is the puzzle. We take the fact; we leave the mystery. If one should affirm that the whole universe came out of God as vapor from the sea, the difficulty is only increased. This is the same as putting to death the Divine Being, and then making the universe his tombstone. The creation of the first man is really a prophecy of the God-man. In that first man is seen the Creator in the creature, the Divine in the human. The first man was supernatural—he was a miracle. Let God become man, and the act would be no more than supernatural, no more than a miracle.

Man really thinks of God in two ways. On the one hand, he is thought of as an infinite Spirit; on the other hand, he is made to appear human-like. Whatever objections some may have against the doctrine of an incarnation of God, these objections really avail nothing, because every man, who thinks of God at all, throws around him a human drapery. Language is proof of that. Let an essay be written respecting the Divine Being, and that essay will have words which imply the human; there is a *figurative* incarnation. Those who cannot bear the thought of an incarnation, sometimes run to the utmost length in their figures of speech. Take the following: "The Infinite Mother spreads wide her arms to fold us to that universal breast, ready to inspire your soul."* Here is a figurative God-woman! This

* Theodore Parker's "Sermons of Religion," p. 392.

is metaphor run mad. The human reason may affirm that God is formless, yet the common working of the mind will bring him down into a sphere of being where he is made to assume form. Whether this be right or wrong, it is a fact of mind. God does appear as divine-human; mentally there is a God-man. This two-fold method of viewing the Deity is seen in the Bible. With one utterance, "God is a Spirit;" with another, "the Lord is a man of war." "He is the high and lofty One that inhabiteth eternity," yet "he is not far from every one of us." Now the statement is, "I am the Lord, I change not;" and again, "it repented the Lord that he had made man on the earth." Indeed, while the Bible gives us the most exact ideas respecting God, yet a cold, abstract Deity is not to its taste. God is brought near to us in everything. The highest theology is made practical, and it appears in a human dress.

We sometimes say that man wants a *person*. The thought is correct. There is not a man that lives but that inclines to a person. The child leans on the bosom of the parent, and the parent lives in the advancing life of the child. The scholar looks to the teacher, the subject to the ruler, and the friend to the friend. But after all, a mere human person does not match the totality of man's nature. There are divine wants that are not satisfied. To satisfy these, sometimes man has gone to men, thinking of them as great, as wise, yea, as divine. Hence nations and races have had their heroes, poets, orators, statesmen, philosophers, priests and prophets. The hunger of souls not yet appeased, they have deified the dead. Driven to desperation, not willing to go where they ought to go, nor do what they ought to do, they have even made the whole universe divine. Reaching this height, personality is lost, God is lost; and a vast Something to take the place of God is all that remains. But all have not acted in this way. Wanting a person of matchless worth, some have thought of the Eternal One himself. There is great power here. The fact cannot be questioned. Yet God standing alone and man standing alone, the soul falters, trembles, turns pale. The vastness of the Deity is oppressive. The purity of an infinite Presence strikes souls dumb. Direct and absolute Divinity has a tendency to consume the creaturely mind. The glory needs to be softened, shaded, lessened and lowered to meet man. One who is divine and human is the central demand of the soul.

As we look through the Old Testament, we are arrested by what seems like an appearance of God in human form. After Adam and Eve had sinned, "they hear the voice of the Lord God walking in the garden," and they make an attempt to hide themselves from his presence. The fair inference here is, that the Divine had a human dress. Three persons appear to Abraham. They all have the human form, so that they are supposed to be three men. One of these differs from the other two. This one is called Jehovah. Here is Jehovah, then, in the form of man. Again, while Jacob is returning to his father's house, a mysterious visitor draws near to him on a certain night. This strange being is called a man; and Jacob wrestles with him till daybreak. It is evident, however, that he was more than man; for Jacob says, "I have seen God face to face, and my life is preserved." At another time, a lofty personage appears to Moses. He is styled "the Angel of the Lord." He is also called Jehovah, God, the Lord God, I Am. An Angel is spoken of as the leader of the children of Israel. This was doubtless the same divine person that appeared to Moses; for the people are charged to obey his voice, not to provoke him, inasmuch as he will not pardon their transgressions. To pardon sin is an act of God. Still, again, Daniel saw in vision "one like the Son of man." "And there was given him dominion, and glory, and a kingdom, that all people, nations, and languages, should serve him." The implication here is that this was a divine man. Thus, without farther specification, we meet with the human element in connection with God.

But let us just glance at what may be called the *medial* principle in nature. What is the universe but a medium through which we learn something about God. Indeed, everything seems to be carried forward upon the medial principle. What is there that we reach directly? Man himself is mediatorial: the type of what is above him; the culmination of what is beneath him. The soul reaches the outer world through the medium of the body; while the body itself in its whole working is dependent upon a most intricate system of medial relations. Mediation is linked to mediation, running through the entire being of man. There are wheels within wheels to such an extent that the mind is baffled in its efforts to comprehend such an intricate system of dependency. If we look to any creature, the same fact of mediation is apparent. It interpenetrates the whole kingdom of creaturely existence, from the animalcule to the archangel. Even the vegetable realm is arranged upon the same principle; and simple inorganic matter has the same characteristic. To a thoughtful mind this principle of mediation is exceedingly suggestive. Is it not possible that even in the Godhead there may be found this medial arrangement? May not the all-connecting principle of mediation in nature be both an echo and prophecy of a mediatorial movement in the Godhead? To say the least, the thought is reasonable.

May there not be a tendency in the Divine Being towards an incarnation? We know that there is a tendency in God to create, for he has created; and the point is settled that the Infinite One will never exist without a creation. To God it is better to have a universe than not to have one. The divine ultimate end is self-manifestation. Such a chief end is desirable; it is worthy of God. Since his design is to manifest himself, why should he not become incarnate? The treasures of the Godhead could be unfolded in a more complete manner by an incarnation than by any other means whatever. "The only true conception of God is one which, so far from being incompatible with, involves his being determined to an incarnation, by his own eternal moral nature; and any conception of humanity is false, which, either in a spirit of defiance or a spirit of pusillanimity, would regard the tabernacling of God in man as a thing either unnecessary or too lofty."*

The most characteristic conception of man is, that he is a *want*; of God, that he is a *fulness*. The one hungers: the other satisfies the hunger. Man wants an incarnation: God is eager to provide an incarnation. The idea of Luther touching this matter, as expressed by Dorner, is the following: "The deity is the subject of a motion out of itself, which, without involving the loss of itself, desiderates humanity as its goal or object: humanity no less is the subject of a like yearning after God or the Word. In the one case, humanity is the 'forma' which God, as the 'materia,' lovingly

* Dorner, "Doct. of the Person of Christ," Divis. ii. vol. i. p. 12.

seeks: accordingly, God not merely has flesh or humanity, but becomes and is man. In the other case, humanity is the 'materia,' which longs for the deity as its goal, even as matter desires and strives after its form; and, accordingly, man becomes God. Both, humanity and deity, remain what they were, and yet they become what they were not; but each, agreeably to its inner yearning, becomes that which relatively to each is the other, so that the result in both cases is nothing else than the God-manhood. Naturally the movement is conceived to originate with the deity, not with the humanity." *

If the arguments from God and man alike show the necessity of a divine incarnation, may we not go a step further, and say, that an incarnation is a want of all intelligences throughout the universe? Do not all need an incarnation of God just because they are creatures,—creatures who never can reach an absolute Spirit? This would seem to be so. It is not merely finite man upon earth that calls for an incarnate Deity, but it is finite mind everywhere. The training of all worlds prior to an incarnation may be but the training of infancy.

* "Doct. of the Person of Christ," Divis. ii. vol. ii. p. 75.

When the fullness of time comes for the God-man to appear, then begins the period of manhood. The grand ideal of life in man is that it be divine and human; and, perhaps, the grand ideal of life in God is that it show itself in one who is divine and human. The incarnation of God thus becomes the basis of a universal theology; and that without which a universal philosophy is impossible. It is the central doctrine of the universe; the royal way that leads to God.

Would there be an incarnation of God if there were no sin? We are inclined to think that there would. An incarnation is necessary to bridge the gulf that separates the Infinite from the finite, and equally necessary to form the medium of a high divine manifestation. It seems fit and proper that there should be One at the very summit of creation who shall be the exact counterpart of God, and who shall at the same time represent in himself the highest form of creaturely life. All created intelligences could then look up to him as the model; he would be the prince of spirits; the crown and glory of the universe; the one great archetypal Being. "The question, whether Christ would have assumed the nature of man if there had been no sin, was not discussed until the middle ages, being started, as it appears, for the first time by Rupertus, Abbot of Duitz, in the 12th century." He says, that "men and angels were created for the sake of the one man, Jesus Christ; he, the head and king of all elect angels and men, did not need sin in order to become incarnate." Wessel adopted the same view. "In his opinion the final cause of the incarnation of the Son of God is not to be found in the human race, but in the Son of God himself. He became man for his own sake; it was not the entrance of sin into the world which called forth this determination of the divine will; Christ would have assumed humanity even if Adam had never sinned." Raymund Lulli says, that "the incarnation is indeed a work of free love; and that we cannot say that it was only brought about by sin, but that God owed it to himself." *

There are two objections to the above, which may just be glanced at. *First,* it is thought that a *theophany* is necessary in a holy universe, but not an incarnation. No doubt a theophany has its place in the system of God.

* Hagenbach, "Hist. of Doctrines," vol. ii. pp. 53, 54.

It forms a connecting link between the creature and the Creator. Still it is a question whether it is not simply a preparatory measure, designed to pass away when a more perfect method has been adopted. A theophany has a degree of vagueness about it. A man *seems* to stand before you, but no man is there. A theophany is impersonal. This is one great objection to it. What the kingdom of mind wants is an exemplar to whom it may look, and a divine-human head to complete the creation and connect that creation with God. A theophany also lacks durability. To-day it may be in existence; to-morrow it may not. Besides, it can never be more than a means to an end. It is thus one-sided, and coldly instrumental. A God-man is both means and end. He unfolds the glories of Deity; yet is worshipped by all creatures, and is forever happy in the exercise of a life that is divine and human. *Secondly*, it is said that an incarnation pre-supposes the *humiliation* of God, which cannot be deemed a requirement of sinless mind. The following things should be noted: A divine man, in a perfectly holy system, would have no weakness of bodily nature; the servant-form would not be his; he would neither suffer nor die; *the* man simply he would be. Certainly the stoop of Deity is not nearly so great when these facts are taken into the account; not nearly so great as when laying hold of a lapsed and lost race in order to save them. Is it possible for us to conceive of any objective movement of God whatsoever without beholding in that a degree of condescension? I apprehend that the Supreme Majesty had to humble himself when he called into existence the first particle of matter that settled upon the bosom of space. The fact of divine humiliation is written upon the whole face of nature, and different degrees of it strike the mind that attentively considers the infinite variety of creation. This very fact makes reasonable any bending down of God that necessarily belongs to an incarnation. In so far as God will never be able to show himself as he is, in so far he is humbled. The objections, therefore, do not break up the line of argument that has been adopted.

But man is a sinner; and here is a new call for an incarnation. The guilty mind is afraid of God; dare not approach him; would, if possible, plunge into some unknown depths to escape from his presence. The nature that sinned must be the nature that shall be assumed on the part of God. True it is that man must save man, and equally true that none but God can do this; hence a God-man is needed. As man, by his fall, must suffer and die, so human nature must be taken up into connection with the divine, in order that the God-man must suffer and die for him. If an incarnation was needed independently of the fact of sin, much more is it needed when sin is a reality. For God to become man for the sake of the fallen, requires a far greater amount of moral power than to become man for the sake of the holy. While sin, therefore, must have an incarnation, love alone can provide it.

The incarnation of God is now a *fact.* "Herein is love, not that we loved God, but that he loved us, and sent his Son to be the propitiation for our sins." The Word that was with God and that was God, "was made flesh, and dwelt among us, and we beheld his glory, the glory as of the only-begotten of the Father, full of grace and truth." Here we have a definite historical statement, which can admit of no dispute. The peculiar form of the New Testament idea of a God-man vouches for its truthfulness. There is nothing like it previous to the advent of Christ. It was not possible for any nation to develop the idea. It was not in a line with the thinking of the ancient world. How could a system of polytheism with its millions of gods, terminate in the incarnation of the one God? How could a system of pantheism, which destroys the Divine Personality, give us a personal God-man? And how could a system of deism, which denies the Divine Trinity, make known the truth that the eternal Son of God was to become the Son of man? To find a footing in such systems for a God-man is impossible. That there were certain disfigured ideas throughout the ancient world respecting incarnations is admitted; but these never could resolve themselves into the true idea.

"The opinion must seem well founded," remarks Dorner, "that the entire vast region of heathen religion contains nothing that can impeach the originality of the Christian ground-idea; whilst, on the other hand, the whole of Heathendom strains after this idea, without being able, from its stand-point, so much as distantly to approach the conception of it in its truth. And the blame, high above all, is due to what has not hitherto been adverted to, viz., that heathenism utterly wants a profound moral view of the world; a defect which also shows itself in the confounding of the consciousness of the world and of God; for thereby also is the ethical idea physically conceived and bedimmed. Ethics includes chiefly the rectitude by which man is put in relation, not only with his fellows, but primarily with God, and so arrives at personality. Thus this idea of rectitude, essential to the ethical, and ever immanent in it, preserves the distinction between God and the world; and without it, love itself would not be love. An idea, therefore, of the unity of the divine and the human, not mediated by the idea of the ethical, can of necessity be only of a physical kind, and superficial, such as we must pronounce that to be which among the Hellenes was consummated in the idea of the beautiful, or of art." "Hence in the whole heathen world the idea of the God-man has never been even remotely approached in the sense in which it always lived in the Church's consciousness."

"Neither does it appear presumptively probable that it is from the spirit of the Hebrew people that such an idea could be derived.

That Jehovah, he who is highly exalted above all that is finite—who, in the sense of forming a conception of him, cannot be seen, yea, the very sight of whom would consume—that he should come down to this world, should put on a finite nature and become man, is an idea which never could have come into the Hebrew religion out of itself."* The truth is, the very *idea* of the God-man is testimony in favor of the fact, for the idea could have no existence save as it sprung from the fact.

If Christ was not divine as well as human, he is a perfect mystery. We sometimes compare one man with another, but Christ can be compared with no one. He cannot even be described. Our ideal of him is deficient. He seems like some new flower that an angel has brought from the skies; planted in the earth, it is more lovely and fragrant than all others; and besides, it never withers or dies, but blooms and smiles with as much beauty amidst the snows of winter, as amidst the finest surroundings of summer. Yea, Christ is like some new star that has appeared in the heavens; and so clear is its light and so radiant its glory, that it stands forth among the stellar

* "Doct. of the Person of Christ," vol. i., pp. 10, 14.

hosts as the central object; and because of its exceeding beauty, men have come to call it the morning star of God. Jesus grew up amidst circumstances that were unfavorable; yet no man, though surrounded with the best circumstances, has made the least approach to him. He was poor; lived among a rude people; had but few educational advantages; was a simple mechanic; yet he stands alone in history. He is a new character. All about him is unique. His ideas of God astonish us —so pure, truthful, perfect. No one could have taught them to him: none had them to teach. He was not made by the past. He seemed to live in a realm of being that was outside of merely human causes. Mark his conception of a religion for the whole world. That is strictly a divine thought. How he speaks also of the soul and its sin, as none could speak when he lived, as none have spoken since he died. Touching the fate of men hereafter, there is such a clearness of statement that we seem to be listening to one who had sojourned in the immortal regions, and had come back to tell us what he had seen and heard. And what is peculiar, he enters into no argument. He utters truth as God would utter it. He speaks with authority, and has no misgiving when he speaks. He never makes any apology; the point that was stated at one time is not corrected at another; experience reveals no mistakes. Respecting his character, that is wonderful. Not in all his life do we see any sign of repentance. He weeps, but never for himself; he is sorrowful, but not because of any lapse of his own. Other men reach piety through penitence; but he is religious without any turning from sin. He is therefore unlike all human beings. Why is he thus different from all other men? If he was simply human, why was he holy? All human beings are sinful—why this single exception? No answer to these questions can be given, if Christ was a man like other men. Evidently he came from a higher sphere. He entered the race from above. God has become man.

Being thus compelled to believe that Christ was divine as well as human, a question meets us just here—was Jesus always conscious that he was divine? It is certain that the human nature of Christ had a beginning. At that beginning the divine was there, for it was the divine that had assumed the human; yet we cannot think that the human nature was conscious that it had been taken up into connection with the divine. The human nature at that first moment had acquired no knowledge. There was therefore no place for either consciousness or memory to act. We have, then, a divine child in existence, yet the child does not know that it is divine. The infant Jesus having begun in this way, it lives and expands, thinking not and knowing not that it has any personal relation to the unbegotten Son of God. It is safe to say that the whole period of infancy was passed in this manner. During what year in the life of Christ the divine began to dawn upon his mind, we cannot tell. Perhaps that which arrested his attention the first, was the fact that he was holy. Inasmuch as he was holy, he was marked off from the entire race of mankind; and in what way could this be explained but upon the ground that he was divine. When Christ had reached the age of twelve, he seemed then to have a realization of his divinity. Those pregnant words, "Wist ye not that I must be about my Father's business?" may teach as much as that. But having grasped the fact that he was divine as well as human, may we not say that the consciousness of the divine was gradual? This gradual consciousness of the divine would be in perfect keeping with the fact of growth that was a characteristic of his human nature. There was therefore an hour in the mental and spiritual life of Christ when the full glory of his divinity touched his creaturely spirit at all points; so that he had a sense of it more complete than had been obtained at any previous time.

There is another question of interest to a thoughtful mind, viz., this, will the incarnation of the Son of God be eternal? From a proper stand-point, the incarnation must be eternal. To say that there is a time coming when the humanity of Christ will cease, is really to say that he never had any humanity in the full sense of that word. Such a view implies that the Logos did not become man; he only took to himself a human *body*. The body therefore can be dropped when the proper time arrives to do so. The incarnation in this way is only a theophany. How very different is this from the truth. Christ was a *man* in the fullest sense of that word. He was born: *men* are born, not bodies merely. He increased in wisdom: a human body and the divine nature could not increase in wisdom. He was tempted:

not God or an impersonal body, but the soul of Jesus. He prayed: does God pray? do bodies offer up supplication? Christ therefore being a true man, there is no possible reason why the incarnation should cease. If all men will live forever, so the man Jesus will live forever.

But some suppose that inasmuch as God became man only for the purpose of redeeming man, so when the work of redemption is ended the incarnation will end with it, there being no further need for it. We do not believe, however, that the Logos assumed human nature simply and only to redeem man. The object aimed at extends beyond salvation; and there is good reason to think that there would be an incarnation even if sin had not existed at all. The end to be gained by the incarnation is endless. The God-man is to be looked upon as the *revealer* and *revelation* of the invisible Deity, necessary not only for one time, but for the whole sweep of eternity. If the humanity of Christ will pass away at the close of redemption, less importance is attached to that humanity than is attached to the individual Christian; for he will live to enjoy God for ever. The opinion has no good foundation.

The God-man will be the centre of heavenly glory to the purified throughout eternity. As he was the object of faith here, he will be the object of praise and adoration hereafter.

CHAPTER II.

DEEP CONVICTION OF SIN: NEED OF A DIVINE SAVIOUR.

THE emphatic thought in the present chapter is not the necessity of a Redeemer, but the necessity of a *divine* Redeemer. Unbelief respecting a doctrine of this kind does not spring so much from the reason, as from the heart. There are many truths which appear quite inexplicable to certain minds, because the affections are in no state to receive them. Yet these same truths are gladly accepted by others, because there is a spiritual want which craves them. The short argument which we here present is purely subjective in its nature. It springs out of the deep consciousness of sin. I would make the oppressive sense of personal sinfulness to be the great receptive state for a divine Saviour.

As a general principle, I only want to know what a man's views of sin are, in order to know his views of redemption. If he has low views of the one, he will have low views of the other. A whole system of theology will have its peculiar shape from the peculiar opinions held touching the doctrine of sin. And this is reasonable; for sin is the great moral disease of the race, and Christian theology is the statement of the remedy with its antecedents and consequents. The consumptive who flatters himself that his system is but a little injured, will not be very anxious to obtain a remedy suited to the nature of his complaint; while another with the same disease, who feels truthfully about himself, will want the best medical assistance he can find. He who has had his house repeatedly plundered feels the importance of having a secure lock for his door, and fastenings for his windows: he who has experienced no trouble of this kind may think it sufficiently safe to be without these. The man who perceives that the ship in which he sails is sinking, will cry for help: his companion who is fast asleep, will be still, fearing no danger. It is according to the same principle that some feel the need of a divine Redeemer, while others do not. Many have no true and deep sense of sin. Themselves being judges, they are not troubled as other men. They do not cry out like the Philippian jailer, "Sirs, what must I do to be saved?"

And it is not a little remarkable, that the sacred theology of conviction has been found chiefly among those who believed that the Saviour is divine. This, be it understood also, not simply among illiterate people, but the educated as well. See what President Edwards says respecting himself: "My wickedness as I am in myself, has long appeared to me perfectly ineffable, and swallowing up all thought and imagination; like an infinite deluge, or mountains over my head. I know not how to express better what my sins appear to me to be, than by heaping infinite upon infinite, and multiplying infinite by infinite. Very often, for these many years, these expressions are in my mind and in my mouth, 'Infinite upon infinite—Infinite upon infinite!' When I look into my heart, and take a view of my wickedness, it looks like an abyss infinitely deeper than hell. And it appears to me, that were it not for free grace, exalted and raised up to the infinite height of all the fulness and glory of the great Jehovah, and the arm of his power and grace stretched forth in all the majesty of his power, and in all the glory of his sovereignty, I should appear sunk down in my sins below hell itself; far beyond the sight of everything, but the eye of sovereign grace, that can pierce even down to such a depth. And yet it seems to me, that my conviction of sin is exceeding small, and faint; it is enough to amaze me, that I have no more sense of sin. I know certainly, that I have very little sense of my sinfulness. When I have had turns of weeping for my sins, I thought I knew at the time that my repentance was nothing to my sin."* Now, it must be noticed that this is not the experience of a simpleton. The person who thus speaks of his depravity had a mind which, for logical keenness and masterly power, has seldom been equalled. What kind of a Saviour, then, does this profound conception of sin call for? Will a human being answer? Is it possible, from the facts of the case, that Jonathan Edwards would have been satisfied with less than an Almighty Redeemer? No: it would have been perfect mockery to have offered him less. The God-man, he would have said, is alone able to help me out of that abyss of sin into which I have plunged. What is thus true of Edwards is equally true of

* Works, vol. i. p. 22.

many other leading minds of history. The entire theological system of Augustine had a subjective grounding. In the language of Neander: "Augustine had learned from his own experience, that, in reference to the know ledge of divine things, the *life* must precede the *conception;* that the latter could only come out of the former; for, in truth, the reason why the simple doctrines of the gospel had, at the beginning, appeared so foolish to him, and the delusive pretensions of that boastful mock-wisdom of the Manicheans had so easily drawn him into its current, was, that those truths had as yet found no point of union whatever in his inner life. It was from the life within that he had learned to believe in these truths, and to understand them."*

It is a significant fact that feeling is an aid to faith. While we fully admit that the objective evidence for the divine in Christ is amply sufficient, we yet know that a thorough conviction of sin has great power to extend the common thinking that relates to his person. No feeling has such a healthy influence as the feeling touching the nature and extent of sin in the soul. With this, man begins to com-

* Ch. Hist. vol. ii. p. 358.

prehend his relation to the Supreme; which fact announces the need of an infinite Redeemer. Wherever there is a dull consciousness of personal guilt, there is always a feeble apprehension of the Divine. Let the moral nature be but once awakened, then the high verities of the God-head appear to the soul. The sin-stricken spirit then looks round imploringly for a divine Mediator. All prejudices and objections flee away, there being nothing for them to feed on. "The practical inquirer," remarks Coleridge, "hath already placed his foot on the rock, if he has satisfied himself that whoever needs not a Redeemer is more than human. Remove from him the difficulties and objections that oppose or perplex his belief of a crucified Saviour; convince him of the reality of sin, which is impossible without a knowledge of its true nature and inevitable consequences; and then satisfy him as to the fact historically, and as to the truth spiritually, of a redemption therefrom by Christ; do this for him, and there is little fear that he will permit either logical quirks or metaphysical puzzles to contravene the plain dictate of his common sense, that the sinless One who redeemed mankind from sin, must have been more than man; and that he who brought light and immortality into the world, could not in his own nature have been an inheritor of death and darkness. It is morally impossible that a man with these convictions should suffer the objection of incomprehensibility, and this on a subject of faith, to overbalance the manifest absurdity and contradiction in the notion of a Mediator between God and the human race, at the same infinite distance from God as the race for whom he mediates."*

But our argument will be more specific, if we notice the several painful emotions that arise in the mind of a convicted sinner.

True conviction of sin has generally connected with it the feeling of *sorrow;* and the more bitter this is, the more urgent the demand for a great Deliverer. The strange solitude and sacredness of penitential grief cry for a divine Helper. Although all sorrow is human, yet somehow or other, it points to the need of the Divine. An argument of this kind can be more easily felt than stated. In so far forth as sorrow is subjective, agitating the deeper heart and deeper soul on account of sin against the Infinite, in so far is there a craving for an

* Works, vol. i. p. 266, Harper's ed.

infinite Saviour, and a shrinking from a mere human one. I scarcely know of a finer or more beautiful argument for the divine in Christ and Christianity than that of sorrow generated because of sin against God. The religion of sorrow is not human: the Redeemer from sorrow is assuredly divine. This element of grief, which takes up its abode in the very centre and soul of human guilt, and which sways to and fro the sin-oppressed spirit of man, is not in general found among the people who live where Christianity is unknown, and is not a common characteristic of the native religions of the race. Natural sorrow springing from the sympathies is universal; mental suffering resulting from sin is found everywhere; self-inflicted torment is a notable feature of the religions of mankind: but pure and simple sorrow for sin is the sole heritage of the pious; lying at the very basis of Christian worship, and at the very beginning of the Christian life. Wherever I see a man, then, cast down in his spirit because of sin, I can point him with confidence to the one divine religion and the one divine Redeemer. That this view is correct, can be seen by any one who will examine the hymns of the

Church which have appeared during the different periods of its history. This kind of literature specially reveals the theology of the feelings. Without quoting testimony, which all can see in their hymn-books, simply notice the following stanza :—

"Some take him a creature to be—
A man, or an angel at most;
Sure these have no feelings like me,
Nor know themselves wretched and lost;
So guilty—so helpless am I,
I could not confide in his word,
Unless I could make the reply,
That Christ is 'my Lord and my God.'"

It is certain also that the *boundless aspirations* of the soul act with unwonted power durring a season of conviction; which fact makes man dissatisfied with less than an infinite Redeemer. The convicted mind runs out with great speed and intensity to the eternal and infinite. Like a bird locked up in its cage, ever desirous to be away to its own native region, so is it with him who has waked up to a consciousness of his captivity. The soul, as never before, is struggling to live amidst the vaster scenes that are beyond it; scenes which become a kind of heritage and home to aspirations; aspirations which find no satisfaction in the mere present tense of human existence. The creaturely spirit, with its divine helps, forms an ideal world of its own into which it enters, and there hopes to find that rest which it vainly seeks for in the rush and roar of earth. The now of mind is always insufficient; its to-day fills not the deep and ever-deepening wants of being; there is a to-morrow needed at whose eternal fountains the soul would drink, and by the aid of whose light, which is everlasting, it would career on in a boundless course; ever ascending the heights of the infinite, it would hope there to find the home of souls, and, finding, abide there forever. We confess ourselves realists enough to believe, that the unquenchable and limitless desires of the soul point upwards to a Supreme Restorer, to a God mighty to save and to bless. That is, the awakened mind will not find peace and rest, the sinful mind will not find pardon and purity, till a Redeemer appears whose higher nature is eternal and divine, though his lower nature had a beginning, and is human.

Another characteristic of a convicted soul is *fear*. He who has never had his mind profoundly agitated and tempest-tossed in view of the punishment of God in eternity, has never yet begun to live. Fear has a judicial element connected with it; and the man, who is thus exercised in his mind, perceives himself standing in the very centre of the divine moral government, with all the woes of the wicked calling upon him to escape to a place of safety. This theology of fear is terrible, but needful to experience. Is it possible that I shall be a lost man forever? Must I run out the line of my being with the moving centuries of hell? No day-star to beckon me away; no morning light to show me the beginning of hope. Must I be lost? How can I help being afraid? How can I sleep to-night unreconciled to God? With all my sin and guilt, and with perdition hard by me, how can I sleep! To-night I may be in hell; many shall be there if I am not. He who has passed through this experience knows what fear is, and knows also how important it is to have a Saviour great with all the attributes of divinity. It is true that a drowning man will seize hold of a straw, and an alarmed soul may be glad to shelter itself the best way it can in any ruined building that appears to offer the least security; but, when it has got there, it only stands shivering with terror, which plainly shows that a more secure and lasting retreat is needed. It is worthy of special attention also that those who believe in but a limited punishment hereafter (thus strangling fear) believe almost invariably in a Christ human, and not divine. This striking fact shows that our reasoning is well grounded. Fear of eternal and divine punishment leads to an eternal and divine Saviour. While if one believes in no punishment at all, he believes in no Saviour at all, divine or human.

Here I would call attention to the fact of *pain* that is connected with deep conviction. The pain is peculiar. I know not that there is any sensation like it. Every man suffers in body and mind. There is a tremendous weight of unhappiness crushing all sinful natures. But all do not experience that mental agony which arises from the clear consciousness of sin. There is a severity and keenness to the pain of conviction not found in the common working of conscience. It would seem almost as if the soul, for the time being, were made to taste the fearful agonies of hereafter; as if the guilty spirit must die a second death before it can rise to a second life. We read of Wilberforce, that "his trouble of soul," while under conviction, "was long and terrible. He asserted in after years that he had never read of mental agonies more acute than his own; and we think it were difficult to over-estimate the weight of this testimony. Yet it was not terror that chiefly dismayed him. 'It was not so much,' these are his own words, 'the fear of punishment by which I was affected, as a sense of my great sinfulness in having so long neglected the unspeakable mercies of my God and Saviour.'"* Now, we cannot but think that, with an experience of this kind, a great Redeemer is needed. The deep wail of the soul, and the answer thereto are convincingly expressed in these words: "O wretched man that I am! who shall deliver me from the body of this death? I thank God through Jesus Christ our Lord."

Still further, in minds oppressed with sin, there is a sense of great *weakness*. Though all be morally weak, yet most men are morally strong. Let one be penetrated with the fact that holiness abides not in any natural soul, that depravity has tainted every stream which once was pure, has withered every flower which once was fair, then he will begin to understand

*Bayne's "Christian Life," p. 169.

how utterly helpless he is. The man who is deeply conscious of his low estate has come to a point where he feels that he must have an Omnipotent Saviour. He stands on no middle ground where he can look both ways with equal indifference; but is rather in a position where he feels that life or death is to be the result. Ask any man who has the feeling of entire helplessness what kind of a Redeemer he wants, and he will answer, as if by instinct, a *divine* one.

Following out the line of our argument to its close, we often find that the convicted sinner has a tendency to *despair;* thus showing the need of a Deliverer of great power. The different steps we have taken lead to this one. First, as the foundation, the soul is deeply convinced of its sinfulness. Secondly, a sadness of heart springs from this. Thirdly, the more lofty aspirations of the soul are quickened in their working. Fourthly, the passion of fear is intensified. Fifthly, the most painful sensations agitate the spirit. Sixthly, there is a strong sense of moral impotency. Lastly, there is a tendency to despair. It is not a little strange that persons, who at other times are quite hopeful in regard to their moral condition and future prospects, should now be just the opposite. To-day they congratulate themselves on account of their goodness: to-morrow they condemn themselves on account of their wickedness. They enter into a cloud, and dwell in darkness. Says Dr. Dwight: "Scarcely any thing more naturally, or more commonly, occurs to the mind in this situation, than doubts, whether such guilt, as itself has accumulated, can be forgiven. *The mercy of God*, which is declared in the Scriptures to be *greater than our sins, to be above the heavens, to extend to all generations, and to endure forever*, is often doubted, so far as the sinner himself is concerned; admitted easily with regard to others, and with regard to all or almost all others, it is still doubted so far as he is concerned, and is easily believed to be incapable of extending to him." "Instead of self-flattery, the only employment which he was formerly willing to pursue with respect to his spiritual concerns, and which he indulged in every foolish and excessive degree, he is now wholly engaged in the opposite career of self-condemnation; and not unfrequently pursues it to an excess, equally unwarranted by the Scriptures." * Some

* "Theology," Serm. 75.

even go so far as to lose their reason; having nothing but despair as a gloomy cloud ever around them, through which they walk as through a perpetual night. Others under the pressure of the feeling, commit suicide; while others still, not going as far as this, are destitute of all hope as long as they live. How many die in utter despair, with nothing powerful enough to lift them up! Now, if this does not call, with a voice so loud that it pierces the heavens, for the greatest possible Saviour, we do not know what meaning to attach to such kind of experience. The whole matter turns upon the strength of motives. The millions of truly convicted men who have obtained hope, have obtained it only by beholding a divine Redeemer.

Such are the thoughts touching this deeply important subject. If in the first chapter we saw that God must become man, we now see that the incarnate God is also a Saviour. Here, we have a *divine person*; there, a *human form*. Here, a *Deliverer;* there, a *Revealer*. This twofold view of God is what man needs. "Whenever the soul is most deeply stirred by penitence, or strained by agony, or kindled into holy aspiration, the spiritual nature craves a more intimate communion with God than would be possible if that God had not mysteriously manifested himself in flesh; not a Sovereign in the skies but a beating and friendly bosom in Bethany. It cries out for the Christ, who, by bearing to us the pity and pardon of the Father, is the Way, and Truth, and Life. The individual heart, when it is really agitated, whether by hope, or love, or pain, or fear, emphasizes the promise of revelation; and the longings of the individual soul respond to the broad verdict of history. It confesses, like Peter before the persecutors, that there is no other name under heaven, given among men, whereby it can be saved." * Each feeling of the convicted soul that we have noticed has really a divine meaning. We are reminded by this language of the feelings, of a language of flowers common among the people of India. Every flower has a sacred meaning. Some speak of peace and rest; others, of sorrow and fear. As each worshipper brings his flowers to the temple, and lays them on the altar, you can almost tell by the beautiful symbolism what the prayer is that ascends to the deity. We may view each feeling of the

* Dr. Huntington, Sermon on the "Divinity of Christ."

troubled spirit as a flower. Each is laid on the altar of God; and a prayer goes up to heaven for that favor of which each is the symbol. The answer to the soul's prayer is Christ.

CHAPTER III.

CONSCIOUSNESS OF GUILT: NEED OF A DIVINE ATONEMENT.

SECTION I.

THE WORKING OF GUILT.

GUILT is one of the most noticeable facts of human nature. It arises wholly from a sense of *sin*. No other evil but sin will produce it. Physical evil may cause me to feel sorrowful: moral evil compels me to feel guilty. Whatever tends to render sin small, tends to render guilt feeble. If the one could be annihilated, so could the other. We do not suppose, however, that any man will ever be able to make himself believe that sin is a mere fancy; because the existence of conscience as the distinctive moral faculty of the soul will keep him from this. There is no amount of sin that can ever destroy the moral nature; and as guilt arises by a law of necessity, wholly beyond the reach of the human will, it must act in the sinful mind forever. And what is worthy of note, it does not merely agitate the mind because evil *effects* follow the commission of sin. The guilt may be intensified when the effects are seen, but yet it is the sin apart from them that originates the guilt. If sin is lost in its consequences, then the suffering is the sin. Moral evil is thus changed to natural evil. According to this, the only thing ultimately to be feared and hated is everlasting punishment. As to the *cause* of sin, it may be said that the simple act of a personal being does not of itself constitute sin; there must be a sinful *quality* pertaining to it before it can be thus characterized. We are to predicate sin of an act when its character is bad; and holiness of an act when its character is good. Unless we thus distinguish, we cannot tell whether the act be right or wrong. Sin is chiefly a lawless, vicious will-not.

The sense of *justice* also connects itself with guilt. Justice is a first truth of the mind. It is therefore universal. It is the safeguard of the business of the world. Without it there would be no certainty. In human jurisprudence, nothing could be done apart from the instinctive justice of the soul. When crime is committed, a million of voices call out for the punishment of the guilty. This is not the cry of revenge, but of righteousness. Even with sins which no human eye beholds, there is found the judicial affirmation—You ought to suffer, you ought to be punished. At the point of the most extreme agony justice says, all is right, misery must follow transgression. The mind has elements in it which may be turned into a world of torture or a world of bliss, according to its state or manner of acting. This juridical concomitant of guilt justifies its existence and heightens its power. The wicked man is now compelled to take sides with God. He is convicted and condemned. He says nothing. The culmination of guilt is *silence.* This feature is not often witnessed in the present life, except among those who fall down before the cross. At the final judgment the wicked will be dumb. The element of justice relates one man to another, and all to God; while it marks off each offender by himself. Silence and suffering are the perfected ingredients of guilt. Speechless despair is the death of souls.

With sin and justice as a groundwork, we may glance at the *retrospective* power of guilt.

It is not present evil alone that the mind is called to contemplate; the evil of the past is made to appear before it. It is true that sin is not always seen, and conscience does not always act. The wheels of the soul move round as usual; nothing special is recognized. Plans of life are laid out. There is a calm in the spirit, and it is busy while it lasts. But a change takes place. Conscience awakes. The sleeping sins of the past startle, and move about. Wherever you go, they go. In silent procession they walk. They look you through. We may reckon with great certainty on the reappearance of the sins of the past. The very nature of subjective punishment would seem to demand this. If some sins must arise to torment the soul, we see not but that all must. Natural retribution will be imperfect upon any other principle. The belief is gaining ground that nothing pertaining to the human spirit is ever lost. "The abstract possibility of an entire restoration of memory, or of the recovery of the whole that it has ever contained, need not be questioned; or if it were, an appeal might be made to every one's personal experience; for we suppose there are none to whom it has not happened to have a sudden recollection,—a flashing of some minute and unimportant incident of early life or childhood; and perhaps after an interval of forty or sixty years. With some persons, these unconnected and uncalled-for reminiscences are frequent and very vivid; and they seem to imply that although the mind may have lost its command over the stores of memory, and may no longer be able to recall at will the remote passages of its history, yet that the memory itself has not really parted with any of its deposits, but holds them faithfully (if not obediently) in reserve, against a season when the whole will be demanded of it. Might not the human memory be compared to a field of sepulture, thickly stocked with the remains of many generations; but of all these thousands whose dust heaves the surface, a few only are saved from immediate oblivion upon tablets and urns; while the many are, at present, utterly lost to knowledge? Nevertheless each of the dead has left in that soil an imperishable germ; and all, without distinction, shall another day start up, and claim their dues."*

The human memory is very much like the historiographer of Oriental monarchs. This

* Isaac Taylor, "Physical Theory of another Life," chap. v.

individual is the keeper of the king's seal; and it is his duty to write down all the king's actions, good and bad. He is to make no change in the chronicle; neither must he introduce any remarks of his own. When his sovereign is dead, it is presented to the council. They read it over attentively. If anything false is found in it, it is erased; if anything has been omitted, it is written out in full. A similar custom prevails in China. All the sayings and plans of the emperor are written in a journal. The document is sealed during his lifetime, and is not opened till his death. It is supposed that a practice of this kind will be for the public good, as it compels the ruler to be on his guard. The volume of memory is to a great extent unknown during the present life of the author. It seems to be written with sympathetic ink, so that its characters do not appear; yet, when they come in contact with the exciting elements of the future state, every letter and word will be visible. After death the book will be opened. "It is a law of mind that the intensity of the present consciousness determines the vivacity of the future memory. Memory and consciousness are thus in the direct ratio of each other. On the one hand, looking from cause to effect,—vivid consciousness, long memory; faint consciousness, short memory; no consciousness, no memory: and, on the other, looking from effect to cause,—long memory, vivid consciousness; short memory, faint consciousness; no memory, no consciousness."* Still further, the more the *will* is brought to bear on memory and consciousness, the more readily and perfectly will any act or state be remembered. If, at the moment one is reading the page of a book, he be thinking about something else, nothing of what has been read will be remembered. The reason of this is manifest,—the *will* was not there to fix the attention. Let the page be read over again, the person *trying* to remember, then, without a doubt, the contents of the book will become the contents of the memory. The same is true of consciousness. I may pass through a strange country and yet see nothing with the soul, because the will does not hold consciousness to the various objects that are around me. If intently I look at everything, I remember. Again, it is worthy of note that *feeling* is generally a matter of consciousness. Let feeling, then, be connected with vice, and

* Sir W. Hamilton's "Metaphysics," p. 256.

the fact must be registered in the mind. Hence, we may expect to see former deeds of darkness lighted into being, by the remembrance of the very feelings that gave them birth. The present pleasure and the present pain of sin are in this way but fuel for the future fires of conscience. With such a view of the subject, the retrospective power of guilt is fearfully significant. The fact that it will be nourished and quickened by a combination of sinful acts and emotions is a terrible feature in the constitution of the human mind.

But guilt is *prospective* as well as retrospective. If it looks back, it looks also forward. There is a storm advancing, and the mind beholds it. There is a dark cloud in the distant horizon where time ends and eternity begins. The marshalling of steeds is heard; the tramp of horsemen falls on the ear. Winged chariots of fire fly through the clouds. Armies are marching along the distant sky and their weapons glisten. At the destruction of Jerusalem by Titus, "chariots and troops of soldiers in their armor were seen running about among the clouds, and surrounding of cities;" even so it is with the anxious, guilty spirit. The imagery of a troubled conscience lines the future. The forces of the Almighty are seen preparing, and the wicked fear and tremble. "The poets and dramatists," remarks Plutarch, "have borne witness to this trait of human nature. Stesichorus represents the guilty Clytemnestra as having a dream, in which a dragon with a bloody head seemed to approach her, presaging the vengeance which Orestes was to take upon her, for murdering his father. They relate of Apollodorus, a monster of inhumanity, that he dreamed that he was skinned alive by the Scythians, and then seethed in a cauldron, from which his heart cried out to him, ever and anon: 'For all this you have to thank me.' Ptolemy Ceraunus had his presentiments of what was to be the end of his career of ambition and blood. His attendants reported to him this singular dream: they saw him arraigned for justice by Seleucus (one of his murdered victims); vultures and wolves acted as judges, and portions of flesh were dealt out to his friends. Such visions, phantoms, oracles, omens, disturb the guilty and admonish them of their doom."*

Now, since guilt has a past and a future, we

* See Biblioth. Sacra, vol. xiii, p. 620.

must notice the peculiar fact that the former suggests the latter in such a way that *both seem to come together in a present.* The moment the curtain is drawn which hides the past, that moment the curtain of the future is torn down, and the man is compelled to stand in the centre, first looking one way and then the other, seemingly without power to help himself, compelled to see both ways, and to swing like the pendulum from side to side, or like the door on its hinges turning evermore. There is, without doubt, a law of association here, finding in some objects a power to suggest the past, while these same objects have a power to suggest the future. A thought, feeling, motive, deed, time, place, person, thing, may each have a *double* significancy, pointing like the magnet both north and south. The flaming torch which conscience carries in her hand, while it reveals the dark background of sin, no less reveals the dark foreground of punishment at the same instant of time! The whole working of this law presents us with a night-scene in the soul. It is like a solitary man going forth with lantern in hand to spy out the ruins of some ancient city. He seats himself on the top of the crumbling wall, lifts up his light, and all around him beholds the remains of ancient greatness,—to the right and left, and on either side, all is open to his inspection. Guilty man thus situated is like a criminal on the highway fleeing for his life. As he looks back, the avenger is in fierce pursuit; as he looks forward, another is hastening to meet him; so there is no escape. Here is a person, we will suppose, who goes forth on some dark night with pistol in hand, designing to attack some passing traveler. It is not long before he meets one. He demands his money. The man refuses. He is instantly shot. The highwayman finds upon the body a purse full of gold, and a silver watch. He hastens with these to his home. As he examines the watch, he perceives that it is the same as that which he gave to his son many years before; and the person he has murdered is his own child! Now, here is an act with a double meaning. That watch as it keeps ticking, tells only of present time; yet, as if some prophetic spirit were moving among its wheels, it points to a son slain, and throws the mind back to that dark hour when the deed was committed. While, again, it points the mind to the future; for that son was sent into eternity by a father.

Thus time and eternity are brought together before the murderer's soul; he must look at both; must read his dark deed and still darker doom. The watch, in fact, reveals the past and the future. The Egyptians symbolized eternity by a serpent with its tail in its mouth. Such would seem to be the fit symbolism of guilt,—a serpent around the soul gnawing it forever.

But a very significant feature of the guilty mind is, that it is *afraid of the Deity*. I am inclined to think that when men have a vivid consciousness of guilt, they have generally some thoughts of a Supreme Power. Guilt is not merely a human affair; in its deepest working it is theistic. At the point of greatest wickedness and wretchedness there are yet conceptions of an Almighty Being, and terrors are awakened in the soul because sin has been committed. There is something peculiar about this. Why should God be feared, any more than any created being? No one has ever seen his face; why then tremble? This, however, is no more strange than that the same soul should look away off upon a coming eternity with fear. It seems obvious that the creaturely spirit is related to a great Sovereign, and to a state of being that has no end. When the wicked man suffers evil in the present life, he is apt to say, "this has come upon me because of my crime." He finds that God is pursuing him, though man may not be able to find his track. And so at every step he fears the Divine Avenger, no less than the human. We see this characteristic brought out distinctly in the brethren of Joseph. They were in Egypt endeavoring to purchase food for their families; but, while there, they are confined for three days; at the expiration of which, we find them speaking in this manner: "They said one to another, we are verily guilty concerning our brother, in that we saw the anguish of his soul, when he besought us, and we would not hear; therefore is this distress come upon us." The mind in this state turns everything that is distressing into a judgment of heaven. It has been said of Voltaire that, without believing in the devil, he saw him everywhere, even where he was not. So those who profess not to believe in God, or those who act as if there were no such Being, fear him though they would not; they assume a bold front, though underneath that is a faint heart. A guilty conscience will sweep away in an instant the sophisms of a life-time Man does fear God. It is a truth of the race. The general sentiment of the heathen world, as it respects the divinity that is over them, is that of fear. It is certainly not that of holy confidence. It were utter folly to speak of familiarity between a guilty soul and a God of absolute purity and justice. The two cannot come together. A just God must be angry, and a guilty man must fear.

SECTION II.

A DIVINE ATONEMENT NEEDED TO MEET THE CLAIMS OF GUILT.

It is seldom that theological writers prove the necessity of atonement from the fact of guilt. The doctrine is generally reasoned out from the nature and demands of the divine moral government. It is our opinion that the argument is only complete when both methods are united. We have then *thought* and *feeling* working together. Says Dr. Chalmers: "The necessity of the atonement experienced as a feeling, is altogether different from the necessity of the atonement conceived of as a notion. To him who is occupied with the feeling, it forms a practical impulse, under which he is led to seek for relief from the distress and the fears of nature ; nor will it be long ere you find him exploring the Bible, and pondering with deep anxiety and attention over the statements which lie before him there. To him who is occupied with the notion, it forms the premise of an argument which he must prosecute to a conclusion, on the side of the doctrine, it may be ; and on which previous verdict it may perhaps depend, whether he will admit the Bible to a hearing on the question at all."* The feeling and the notion present us with two ways of reaching the same important truth. The former we select just now because there is a want to be satisfied.

First, something is needed to *quiet the guilty mind.* How can this be done? If the sinful man is made sinless, will conscience then be at rest? At first sight it would seem so, but yet it cannot be. Suppose that a noted thief and murderer were to flee away to some unknown region, and while living there should become a moral man, would consciousness of guilt with reference to persons plundered and slain be annihilated because of his reformed life? The

* "Institutes of Theology," vol. ii, p. 17.

thing is impossible. He could not fail to have anguish of mind in view of the evil he had done. He is a criminal still, whatever his present moral standing may be. The public well-being, the demands of equity, are not satisfied by the character which he now possesses. Simple purity, then, will not quiet conscience. We have only to grasp the true idea of guilt, in order to see this. How does it arise? It arises on account of transgression of law. Plainly, then, if guilt is to be removed, law must be satisfied. So long as the mind remains as it is, it can have true peace in no other way than this. There is a necessary connection of cause and effect. A broken law the cause—guilt the effect: a sustained law the cause—peace the effect. "The correlate to guilt is atonement, and to attempt to satisfy those specific wants of the sinful soul, which spring out of remorse of conscience, which is the *felt* and *living* relation of sin to law and justice, by a mere provision for spiritual sanctification, however needed and necessary this may be, in its own place, must be like the attempt to satisfy thirst with food."*

* Prof. Shedd's "Introductory Essay" to Coleridge's Works, p. 51.

It is both a natural and supernatural truth, that "without shedding of blood is no remission." The necessity of an expiatory sacrifice, in order to wash out guilt, is strikingly illustrated by a practice among the ancient Phrygians. The man who was to be purified was put into a pit, and over him was placed a platform having innumerable holes pierced through it. On this platform was laid the animal that was to be slain. Through the small holes flowed the blood of the slaughtered beast; and this like rain descended on the head, face, tongue, and body of the guilty man. He received a baptism of blood, by which he was considered purified. Here outward atonement, or satisfaction to law, and inward cleansing went together.

Secondly, a powerful arm is needed to remove the *evils of eternity* which man fears. The boding sense of danger, which leaps out of active guilt, proclaims in emphatic language the necessity of a great Atoner, who is both able to remove the danger and the fear of it. It is not personal guilt only that the soul would be away from, but future evil as well. This stunning fact is too great to be put down with a hush, which is all that some can do; while others not so hardened, yet as ignorant, stand and tremble, unable to go either one way or the other. If guilt can only be removed by upholding the law, fear of punishment can only be removed by the same process. So long as the fear is an effect, and well grounded, there is no way to change it but through its cause. Conscience is not merely individual, having its sin and punishment wholly within itself; it is governmental; hence a punishment without awaits the transgressor. In the first section, we have seen that the sense of justice is inseparably connected with guilt; consequently justice must be satisfied before the alarms of guilt can be dispelled. The early Egyptians were in the habit of branding a seal upon the bull that was to be sacrificed. The figure on the seal represented a man kneeling, with his hands tied behind him, and a sword placed at his throat. How significant the emblem! Surely with the sword of justice held over man, he needs an atonement of priceless value.

Thirdly, a divine Reconciler is needed to *appease God.* Man sins against God, then fears him, and out of this arises the craving for a Mediator. It is because Jehovah is what he is, and all sin is against him, that the mind takes the direction here mentioned. I look upon this Godward movement of guilt as the great subjective basis for a divine atonement. There are two ideas which ground themselves in the mind of sinful man, and which make their appearance when he stands face to face with God; viz., the divine *justice* and *holiness*. The sinful character becomes the more sinful by its contrast with the unsullied purity of the Supreme; and this makes man shrink back out of sight, causing him to feel that he is cut off from the divine favor. And as guilt rises up in his mind, and he beholds the justice of the Infinite One, he fears exceedingly, for vengeance is at hand; and so the great want is an all-sufficient atonement. The grand desideratum is to find that which will uphold the justice and honor the holiness of the Deity; for these are the objective verities which the guilty conscience affirms; and, until they are met and satisfied, there is no such thing as bringing God and man together.

These three points show the *internal* working of the guilt-stricken soul with respect to a system of mediation that can quiet conscience, remove punishment, and pacify God. We now present three other points from the *external* sphere, relating to the same evils and the same remedy.

First, when man has a deep consciousness of guilt, he is prompted to make *confession* of his sin. He supposes that this confession will be pleasing to the Divine Being, will tend to gain his favor, will be influential in easing the mind of its pain. To a certain extent, it will appear to make the sin less than it is; and this is one of the dangerous features of mere confession; showing also that there is no true repentance in it, but simply a manifestation of restlessness. But as something must be done, what more reasonable than free and open confession of having done wrong. To the guilty mind at least, there is something that looks truly penitential in this. The man feels uneasy in regard to his sins, has some sorrow, and a peculiar wish that they had not been committed. The foundation of the whole, however, is fear. There is a vision of the wrath to come and the divine displeasure, compelling the agitated spirit to acknowledge its demerit. But the method adopted does not bring peace, and the woes that intimidate become no less.

Secondly, the man now attempts to make

restitution for the sins of the past. He approaches the point, however, in a gradual way. At first, he breaks off from the more glaring acts of transgression, as these appear to him to be the most wicked. He is also more scrupulous with reference to those duties that are deemed religious. He is beneficent; making attempts even at self-denial; imagining that by the liberal bestowment of money for charitable and sacred purposes, he thereby makes some reparation for the evil he has done. In deeds of this kind there is the appearance of doing more than one's duty; hence a feeling of satisfaction as if the Supreme Rewarder were well pleased with such sacrifices. This feature is seen in the conduct of certain persons in the tenth century who believed the world was about coming to an end, and who, as a consequence, were afraid to appear before God. "Some devoted themselves," says the historian, "by a solemn and voluntary oath to the service of the churches, convents, and priesthood, whose slaves they became, in the most rigorous sense of that word, performing daily their heavy tasks; and all this from a notion that the Supreme Judge would diminish the severity of their sentence, and look upon them with a more favorable and propitious eye, on account of their having made themselves the slaves of his ministers. The opulent attempted to bribe the Deity, and the saintly tribe, by rich donations conferred upon the sacerdotal and monastic orders, who were regarded as the immediate vicegerents of Heaven." * Again, others will adopt rules of penance for themselves, and be more strict in these than in the unchangeable principles of morality. By such a method the conscience is quieted for a time; for there is that about it which looks like an atonement. But the delusion after a season departs, and the old fears return. It is now seen that a moral being can never do more than his duty; that it is absolutely impossible in the nature of things to make amends for the past. Man is obligated to do all he can each moment of life; and, instead of doing more now to make up for the deficiencies of the past, he must do more to meet the demands of the present. All do less than God requires. Something is therefore still wanted to make a true reparation.

Thirdly, the guilty man now offers *sacrifice.* Confession and restitution have failed; an innocent animal must atone for the transgressor.

* Mosheim, Ch. Hist., vol. i. p. 248.

In the history of the race, few things are so remarkable as the fact of sacrifice. Its universality shows that there must be a ground for it in the human mind. Admitting that the system was instituted by the Creator, why was it instituted? Subjectively at least, there is reason for it in the consciousness of guilt, and in the deep cry of troubled natures for a ransom. Solemn and significant it is to see a sinful man going forth with a lamb for a sacrifice. There is an attempt to do away with the schism of the soul; an attempt also to introduce harmony between that soul and God. But a beast without a stain can accomplish no such end. The introduction of human sacrifices shows that man was dissatisfied, and that he was anxious to do his utmost that peace might be restored. These assuredly were not by divine appointment; they were the pure inventions of men,—men driven to madness by the clamors of sin and vengeance. Is the great atonement, then, found at last? It seems not. The fire of the soul was rather made to burn more fiercely; no human blood could quench it. An only child, a spotless virgin, a princely man, were tried; the trial ended in despair. In the language of Porphyry, "There was wanting some universal method of delivering men's souls, which no sect of philosophy had ever yet found out."

Our conclusion, then, is that a *divine Atoner* is demanded. The whole history of religion points to such a person. Heathenism and Judaism culminate in the Crucified. The history of the world is chiefly sacrificial. The worship of heaven is a psalm; the worship of earth a sacrifice. There is "a Lamb slain from the foundation of the world." The course of modern speculation touching this deeply important subject is either towards a divine and glorious Redeemer, or towards a divine and glorious humanity. If Jesus is not exalted and worshipped, the race will be. There is no stopping place between the Sinless and the sinful. The choice is between an atoning Saviour or none at all.

In the three following chapters our point of view is changed. It is supposed that we have discovered the great redemptive person of Christianity, and so stand beside him to learn of his fitness to meet our case as fallen beings. Man is viewed as a transgressor of law, exposed to punishment, oppressed with sorrow; and the God-man is viewed as the One who meets these difficulties.

CHAPTER IV.

THE LAW BROKEN: THE DIVINE SUSTAINER OF LAW.

SECTION I.

MAN A TRANSGRESSOR OF LAW.

THE above statement involves a number of distinct propositions. The one that lies at the foundation is this—man is a *subject of moral law*. We might reason from analogy that man is under law, for nothing thus far has been discovered without it. The elementary atom, the compound grain, the globe, the system, the collection of all the systems into one vast whole, —each and all have a law. In every organic thing we have it; it were impossible to have an organism without it. Man would be a mental, moral, and physical mystery, if he had no connection with it. But the chief idea is not so much that man is under law, as that he is a subject of *moral* law. It is this which brings him into a new sphere, the sphere of moral qualities, and the high realm of the divine. If one wants proof, it is found in human consciousness. We do not theorize; we simply take a fact of the soul. The right and the wrong are affirmed by conscience,—affirmed with great uniformity. This is good, that is evil. The moral law is interwoven with the soul. A denial of inherent subjective ethics is a denial of mind, and, by fair inference, a denial of the Supreme Mind. Then, too, the soul is not merely a thinking, feeling, acting substance; it is all these in the moral, and for the moral. Character is ultimate; thought is not. To love is higher and better than to think.

And what is important to be stated also is this, that conscience is not by any means character; an enlightened conscience does not constitute a good man. As it respects God, law is the expression of his holiness; the divine law is the free utterance of the divine rectitude. The fact that God is love, makes him a law to himself and to all intelligences. We cannot speak of man in this way. The pure spirituality of the soul has taken its flight. The nature where holiness ought to be is withered and dead; yea, sin has taken its place; for, if a faculty or power has not the good for which it was made, it will have the evil. The soul, as now it stands, has its law of right; but it has, with significant contrast, its heart of wrong. The utmost that man can have now is a cold virtue; for the fire that once burned on the altar of the soul is extinguished, and the love that once ascended to the Infinite is now no more. I am afraid that many of our ethical writers forget this. Conscience may be followed in an ethical way, yet the righteousness which God approves is not thus found. I can conceive of a man toiling with utmost constancy for the amelioration of the race at the bidding of conscience, and yet, though satisfying himself, not satisfying him who knows the heart. There are not wanting commandment-men, and even sympathetic men; but the greatest want of the age is *sanctified emotion and action.* "If the approbation of conscience," says President Edwards, "were the same with the approbation of the inclination, of the heart, or the natural disposition and determination of the mind to love and be pleased with virtue, then approbation and condemnation of conscience would always be in proportion to the virtuous temper of the mind; or rather the degree would be just the same. In that person who had a high degree of virtuous temper, therefore, the testimony of conscience in favor of virtue would be equally full: but he that had but little, would have as little a degree of the testimony of conscience for virtue, and against vice. But I think the case is evidently otherwise. Some men, through the strength of vice in their hearts, will go on in sin against clearer light and stronger convictions of conscience, than others. If conscience's approving duty and disapproving sin, were the same thing as the exercise of a virtuous principle of the heart, in loving duty and hating sin, then remorse of conscience will be the same thing as repentance ; and just in the same degree as the sinner feels remorse of conscience for sin, in the same degree is his heart turned from the love of sin to the hatred of it, inasmuch as they are the very same thing." *

But without enlarging upon this thought, let me here notice the *laws* or *limitations* of conscience. As the human mind has three grand divisions, viz., the faculty of thought, feeling, choice, conscience must extend to each and all of these if it is to be the proper guide

* "The Nature of Virtue," chap. v.

of man. 1.—The decision of conscience respecting duty is conditioned by the *decision of the understanding*. It is on account of this peculiar law of conscience that we see such a great diversity among mankind touching the right and the wrong of certain actions. What is considered morally good in one place, is considered morally evil in another. A course of action may seem right to a person to-day, while to-morrow it may seem wrong. Unless we make the moral faculty to be a soul by itself, it must lean upon the understanding. This, in fact, is a noble characteristic; for thereby man stands out before the universe as a reasonable being. It throws also a vast responsibility upon him. He must do his best to know what duty is to himself, to men around him, and to God. If through indolence, prejudice, or sinful inclination, man will not strive to gain the truth, he is to blame for that. Whatever may be the opinion which he forms, he is accountable. If conscience is not enlightened, if it is led astray by that which is false, man is guilty. The moral reason can thus try and condemn the very faculty on which it depends. 2.—It is a law of conscience that it can pronounce a decision upon the *states of the heart.* The very life or death of souls is found here. If the current of the affections is towards God, it is good; if towards self, it is bad. The least aversion with respect to God and goodness is sin: the feeblest emotion of love to the pure and the divine is holiness. Yea, if the heart is wholly in a negative state, is without goodness, that state is sin. Conscience reaches down to the positive and the passive alike. The moral faculty is perfected and satisfied when God and love are enthroned in the heart. 3.—*States and individual acts of the will* are good or evil. We believe that there are two movements of the human will. One movement begins with the first sin; at which point it encircles the whole moral nature of the soul, acting with the utmost constancy, never changing for a moment, continuing through all eternity unless arrested by divine grace. This permanent, voluntary state is the one great sin of the soul. This is the life-sin of all unrenewed men. By such a tremendous sweep of the will, the whole being is led off from God. If this state is changed, however, as it is in conversion, then, it is approved by the conscience. The spiritual drift of the angel mind and the divine mind is holy, while that of fallen spirits is unholy. The second movement of the will is that which is seen in individual volitions. All the thousand acts that are done each day are good or evil. Thus we behold conscience going out to the threefold nature of man,—to the intellect, the affections, the will. The one personal being is now approved or condemned.

We turn to consider our next leading proposition, viz., the *obligation of man to keep the law.* There is an imperative in the soul, supreme and final, above all the demands of appetite, passion, desire, emotion, which man feels he ought to obey. This obligation has for its basis the *right*, and that alone. Man has not to search out the eternal consequences of things before he can ascertain his duty, for this never could be done by a finite being. He has not to tell the number and degree of pleasurable sensations which an action might produce before he can be prevailed upon to do it. Just as if that action which tickles the most were the best. A beastly morality this would be. One must do good because it is good; he must abstain from evil because it is evil. It is duty, not pleasure. The sphere of the ought is rectitude. We must regard it as in the conscience, not in the blind feelings. Take it away from this part of the soul, and we have no obligation at all. The mere sensitive nature is aimless; has no power to command; cannot lead to the right. Obligation is in the line of moral law; in the line of unchangeable principle; in the line of good now and forever. It is a primary and not a secondary truth. And just so far as one acts for the right is he to be deemed virtuous. The man who only keeps from killing one because he would be hung if he committed the deed, deserves no credit; he is guilty at heart. He who only can be prevailed upon to assist his neighbor in distress by the combined motives of self-interest and pity has no goodness. That action is alone pure which has the moral nature going out to it because of its intrinsic goodness. Whether we take notice of it or not, this is really the way we judge of actions. We measure a man by his disinterestedness. Hence the effort of many to *appear* benevolent, while at heart they are not. Only let a person tell us that he is wholly selfish in his acts, which look benevolent to us, and we instantly condemn him. It would seem, then, that all men, whatever their theories, really believe that obligation is founded on right, and on that only. Notice now the laws of obligation.

1. Before I can be obligated to do a thing, I must have the *moral law*. Each man has this written on the substance of the soul. It is not necessary that God should write his law on tables of stone in order to make man accountable. Obligation might be increased by this means, but not created. The whole world, independently of the written word, are under law.

2. There must be *freedom of will*. "Were it not for this conscious freedom, man would be incapable of government or obligation. Some, indeed, would object that the possession of such a power would render him incapable of government. Superior to the government of compulsion and necessity, such as that to which matter is subject, it certainly does render him. But not incapable of rational and moral government; for it leaves him open to the government of motives. And it is the consciousness of his power to deal with this influence freely, as opposed to its necessitating force, that lies at the foundation of his sense of responsibility. To say that any moral obligation could rest on a creature whose actions are determined by

necessity, would be a self-contradiction. If my volitions are truly, and in every sense, necessitated, the divine jurisdiction in my breast cannot commence till after I have willed."*

3. A great law of moral obligation is, that it cannot be limited by time, it is *eternal.* We discover this law by considering the nature of right, and the nature of mind as related to that. Since I am obligated to do a thing because it is right, I must be obligated forever, inasmuch as the right cannot change. Right from its nature is *perfect;* consequently it must remain the same throughout the whole sweep of endless duration; and obligation is thus stamped with the same perpetuity. Simple mind also will be the same forever; hence it must have an imperative running on co-extensive with its existence. I do not, of course, mean that the mind will be the same in development throughout the boundless future, but that it will be the same in *nature;* the same faculties that constitute mind to-day will constitute mind a million of ages hence. On this account, wherever a soul is obligated to do right now, it is obligated always.

4. Obligation will *increase forever* in propor-

* Dr. Harris, "Man Primeval," p. 112.

tion to the soul's *possible advantages*, and *possible development* from these. This is a reasonable law. Whatever God has placed within the reach of mind, there is obligation to seize hold of it, and to have a corresponding development on account of it. If there be higher light and higher influence than the mind can gain, that ends the matter; the limit is the possible, and not the impossible. If, however, the means which God has designed for the growth of the soul be misused, or not used at all, and there be no growth, then what could have been, and ought to have been, will be the measure of accountability. Obligation to right demands as much as this. It cannot take less; for if it could, it would destroy itself, and cease to be obligation. The grand law is, increase forever according to the ratio of the possible. Any excuse thrown in for the breach of law avails not, for wrong never can be excused; if it could, the wrong would be changed to right, and being right, no excuse would be needed.

5. The next law of obligation is, that it limits itself to the *relations in which one may be placed at any given time*. If one is a parent, he stands in a certain relation to his family,

and has certain obligations growing out of this which he would not have if he were not a parent. If one is translated from the province of a mere private citizen to some official station in life, he has new obligations by reason of the new relation in which he is placed. A constable is not required to perform the duties of a sovereign, nor a policeman those of an ambassador. Each individual has a series of relations running along with the years and circumstances of life, which relations limit the obligation. Or if the relation in which one finds himself be not changed for another, but only enlarged, then, for that enlargement, we have obligation. These five laws, we think, cover the whole ground.

It remains for us to notice the fact that man has *broken the law.* To break law is to keep law, yet not in the same sense. If one loves, he hates: if one hates, he loves. Man will have an object for the affections, good or bad; he will have a law for the mind, sinful or holy. To be vacant, isolated, aimless, is not the condition of the human soul. God so created man that he must have a centre towards which he will turn; he must have a supreme commander that will bid him go and come. The true philosophy of sin is seen in this, that the ends, objects, and states of mind peculiar to holiness are changed, or turned completely round. An attentive mind can see, in all the movements of a fallen creature, the ultimate end for which he was made, and the course of life he ought to pursue. The reign of sin and death suggests the reign of holiness and life. He who sees hell cannot fail to think of heaven. It is quite apparent that although man has broken the law of God, he yet has subjected himself to another law. The change that has been wrought in the soul by moral evil has necessarily called into being a *law of sin.* This is loved and obeyed. It is at this point that we begin to see the true nature of transgression. Sin is perfected when it has a law; doubly perfected when that law is constantly obeyed. God now is utterly rejected. There is a sovereignty in the existing depravity which will allow no interference. When unlawfulness becomes law, sin culminates.

The entire cycle of human existence is now by itself; man is working out his plans in a sphere separated from the great spiritual impulse of the Deity. This cycle of fallen souls is that of mere nature. All men have dropped down from the supernatural realm, and are acting on a plane of being towards the earth, —cold, cheerless, dead. Sometimes there is a struggling of soul when man realizes that he is thus exiled from God. This struggling arises from the motion of latent ideas and lost rays of the divine that still remain in the fallen mind. The fire that once burned on the altar of the heart left behind it ashes with sparks here and there, that now and then manifest their presence by a movement of unrest, a sigh of the soul, a secret, hidden pain, a struggle in the line of moral goodness, and sometimes an effort to turn round, but yet with no holy desire for it. Man has, on certain occasions, dreamy and indistinct thoughts of the higher world of being to which he once belonged, but from which he has fallen; and so his present nature-life does not satisfy. At such moments, with the aid of his reason and conscience, he will set agoing a process of gradual reformation. He carries himself along with a simple ethical life; he moves the outer edge of his being; while the great central sweep of his character is never less than before; that still keeps within the dread cycle of death and darkness. Sin against God, whatever the turnings of the soul, is never reduced, but ever increased. God is still opposed ; self is still followed.

There is an *outgoing* influence connected with sin. What a strange system that would be where each being was isolated ; influencing none, influenced by none ; a mighty collection of intellectual atoms with no affinity ; simply a heap of passionless monads ! Such is not the system which the All-wise has chosen. The sin of the archangel who fell in heaven lives to-day among earth's millions ; and among the subsequent generations of time it will live still, even to the last ; sin has no last. It would seem, with some great principle of generalization before us, as if the whole universe were related. One almost thinks that there are echoes of sin which can be heard throughout the most distant regions of creation ; vapors of evil that may ascend to the very atmosphere of heaven, causing for a moment a commotion as they pass to spheres beyond. It is certain, at any rate, that kindred minds who are fallen move and turn each other. A principle of disorder has been introduced into spiritual natures, which makes one being strike against the other.

We now reach the important thought that man is *demeritorious for not keeping the law.* "Our moral convictions declare that sin is of evil desert, condemnable, punishable. This conviction is of precisely an opposite character to that which we entertain in regard to good affection and action. We declare the sin to have in itself evil desert; we condemn it in consequence, and we say of it, that it should be discouraged, nay, punished. The very ideas, so full of meaning, involved in these mental convictions, are native, original, and necessary. We cannot get them from mere sensations of pleasure or pain, or from any intellectual operation whatever; and yet we are constrained to take this view of sin wherever it is pressed fairly upon our notice. It is this conviction that stirs up and keeps alive a sense of guilt and apprehension of punishment in the breast of every sinner. It is found even among children, and among the rudest and most ignorant savages, who are urged thereby to try some means of avoiding or averting the wrath of God, and who are prepared in consequence to listen to the parent, or teacher, or missionary, when he speaks of the desert of sin, and points to the Saviour who suffered in our room and stead, and so made reconciliation for transgressors."*

SECTION II.

THE GOD-MAN A SUSTAINER OF LAW.

If we would understand the essence of atonement, we must understand the essence of law. Whatever we make the one we necessarily make the other. If the law be nothing but a cold abstraction, the atonement will partake of its nature,—it will look like it. If on the other hand it is inseparably connected with personal being, guiding and measuring the moral life of souls, or expressing the holy tendency of the divine mind, then, it is a living, beautiful reality, imaging forth the nature of that device which must be introduced into the system of God, in order to sustain it. Law personified and acted out is love; lawlessness is hatred. The scheme, then, which is designed to uphold law must have love for its great characteristic. It is impossible to

* McCosh, "Intuitions of the Mind,' p. 301.

satisfy it with anything short of this, for law knows nothing but love. Whether I look to honoring justice or holiness, government or God, it makes no difference, love, and that alone, must do the work. This view compels me to look upward to that great Being who is love itself, and compels me to see that redemption for my soul can never be wrought out save by an infinite act of love. Under a system of human law this loving characteristic is not deemed necessary, inasmuch as human law is mainly external; but under the divine law outward conformity is nothing, — "Love is the fulfilling of the law." Whether it be in the sorrow that agitated the soul of the Innocent, or in the suffering that rent his lofty being, it was the love that sorrowed and the love that suffered from the cradle to the cross. "He was obedient in acting and obedient in suffering; but his acting was an act of suffering, and his suffering the highest voluntary act. He drank the cup which his Father gave him; but his meat and drink was to do the will of his Father. While he was like sinners in all things, sin excepted, in the active obedience of his life he bore the penalty of sin, even death;

and the final death-struggle was nothing else than the consummation of his suffering activity; 'he was obedient even unto death.' And though he drank this cup with deliberate love, since it was his Father's will, yet was this suffering also his highest act of voluntary obedience."* I can find no word that gives such meaning to the redemptive mission of Jesus as the word love. If he endured a single pang or performed a single deed in order to uphold law which was not characterized by love, I know not where to find it. We doubtless fail on account of the habit we have cultivated of exclusively contemplating the *atonement* instead of the *Atoner*. We seem evermore to be thinking of a work, and not of a person. A refined system of idolatry has led us to adore the symbol, instead of the Saviour. The tendency of the philosophical mind to abstract thinking has led to a separation of the remedy from the Redeemer. The divine law is sustained by divine love.

First, the love which sustains the law that man has broken is *unique* in its character. I mean by this to affirm, that it could only have been conceived and carried out by a divine

* Tholuck, "Guido and Julius," p. 143.

person. It is a new thing in the universe; it is a new method of honoring law. The human reason may examine its claims when once the divine fact appears, but it has no power to go back of this. The redemptive love of the God-man stands very much in the same relation to finite mind as the existence of sin in the universe. No superior intelligence would ever imagine that moral evil would be allowed to darken any world of the divine system; and, after sin had found a place in the dominions of the Creator, none would suppose that he would descend to earth, and there with loftiest love sustain the law which man had broken. Human sin and divine love are beyond the reason of mortals. Faint types of the Christian remedy may be seen here and there, but nothing just like it has occurred or will occur in the onward march of history. There is no doubt a law of progress in the universal system of the Infinite which makes certain the advent of some great Deliverer, yet it is questionable whether the whole truth respecting his person and mission would enter any mind prior to his coming. When once we have found the first man, we may go backward among the centuries and inhabitants of the geologic earth, and there see anticipations of an intellectual dynasty that must begin at the close of the great working week of the Almighty. So in like manner when once we behold Eternal Love coming under the conditions of time and place, entering into humanity, and forming a part of its history, we may, with such a light around us, see, through all the past, hints and prophecies of a new redemptive age centering in "the second man, the Lord from heaven." Aside from this, all is uncertain and unsatisfactory. The Redeemer is wholly a mystery of love. "The *mode* of achieving salvation," remarks Henry Rogers, "though we cannot, *à priori*, speculate on it, was the result of a great moral necessity, which Love was resolved to confront since it could not evade it. And hence it is that so many millions, won and vanquished by this spectacle, have declared (and this is the only just influence of the doctrine) that it is the atonement which has chiefly furnished them, as with hope and peace, so with the strongest motives to revere justice, to obey law, to 'go and sin no more.'" * And what lends peculiar significance to this exalted method of sustaining law is the likelihood

* The Greyson Letters, p. 236.

that as it is *original*, so it is also *final*. Such an exhibition of superior benevolence will doubtless never again astonish the inhabitants of any world, nor smile along the years of any age of a deep futurity. It forms a special intervention of the Deity in behalf of a rebellious province of his empire, never to be repeated, but to stand forth as a stupendous memorial throughout eternity, claiming the admiration of all intelligences. This feature seems to augment, if possible, a love which already is infinite, and seems to make a violated law doubly secure and doubly honorable. Nothing more than this could any one wish; nothing better could any one claim. The law is upheld by a miracle of love.

Secondly, *no finite being could demand as his due* the manifestation of this peculiar love. God was not the debtor of the universe; neither man nor angel could demand the performance of such a work of benevolence. The idea never entered any mind that such a love was even possible; consequently there could be no thought of claiming it. This fact shuts the door of obligation at once. Common law cannot claim atoning love. Indeed, law throughout the universe asks no more than the usual sinless obedience of accountable beings. There is an element of sacrifice and self-denial quite apparent in the love of Christ, which cannot of right be demanded of any of the pure intellects of heaven. I can see no other way than to place this great righteousness of the Redeemer in a sphere by itself. Although he lived upon the earth, he also lived upon a plane of being far above the earth, and entirely distinct from that which marks the common life of pure spirits. It would seem as if this high Ransomer came forth at the bidding of some transcendental law of his own nature. His love was such that, all things considered, it seemed best to erect a theatre before the universe; best to act out a life wholly like himself, that thus the law might be established which man had broken. In this way the whole redemptive act is a feature of the higher sphere of Mind. It is purely supernatural from beginning to end. What the finite could not claim, the Infinite could. That which may be called the great law of the atonement had its origin in the law of the Godhead. Love was the reason and love was the act. The voluntary tendency of the divine nature was towards Calvary. This prepared the atonement; this carried it out to a completion. It might almost seem as if the law were honored, in part, by the simple existence of redeeming mercy in the Godhead, while as yet it had not been manifested in the person of Christ. And, surely, if the law is thus dignified by the antecedent movement of love, much more is it by its subsequent movement. At any rate, it seems quite certain that the princely benevolence of Jesus adds greater dignity to law and greater glory to God, than a mere system of pardon which has no atonement. "That human nature might be restored, or any portion of mankind be eternally saved unto the glory of God, it was necessary that an *obedience should be yielded unto God and his law* which should give and bring more glory and honor unto his holiness than there was dishonor reflected on it by the disobedience of us all."*

Thirdly, Christ upholds the law by a love which is *inimitable*. Viewing the life of Jesus from a human stand-point, we may say that all should imitate it. He is the great pattern of the race. But when we view that wonderful life as but the process of love in time for the sustentation of law, then we affirm that it

* John Owen, Works, vol. i. p. 200.

cannot be imitated. It is impossible for any created being to act over again *atoning love.* It does not come within the sphere of the finite. A new plane was struck out purposely by it, and purposely for it. We must of necessity have a God-man passing through scenes of sorrow and woe, before we can have even the groundwork of such a love. And as we have noticed, it is not even probable that the Deity will manifest again such strange benevolence. The sacrifice is too mighty ever to be repeated. An unspeakable importance thus attaches to it. Its inimitable character loads the universe with profit and the law with honor. The whole significance of the point before us is seen just here, that Christ had a supernatural existence and a supernatural benevolence. He came among men from above, and not according to the common course of nature; he lived among them as human, and yet he was divine. He formed thus a kind of parenthesis in the history of time and eternity. Though as man he was conditioned by laws of human development, his spiritual consciousness was none the less redemptive; for he was God as well as man. He had what may be called an atoning experience. Made under the law like others, he could not forget that he was unlike all men in that he was the vicarious Upholder of law. He was living not with exclusive reference to himself, but with reference to the world he came to save. Hence he viewed sin and its punishment, God and his government, not as man, but as Mediator.

These mere hints are suggestive. There is a wondrous height and depth connected with the life of Christ. We find no satisfaction in viewing him simply as the good man, the exemplar of the race, the reformer of the world. His merely human position in history is beautiful, attractive, perfect. Yet the human to us is great because the divine is there with it. His life, as no other, was a life of God. For our part, we cannot understand the unparalleled love of Jesus unless we give an *atoning* significance to it. When we see that he was acting evermore with reference to a law that man had broken, was preparing a righteousness which might be made available in law for the justification of the believing sinner, then all is clear and satisfactory; but all is confused and inexplicable without this. It is easier to believe that his love was redemptive, than that it was like that manifested by any other pure mind.

"Who that is acquainted with the nation, fanatical, rough, vicious, and indocile, toward which he exhibited such love and forbearance; who that knows the danger with which he was daily threatened, and the snares laid with so much art to entrap him; who that reflects upon the ingratitude with which he was treated, the contempt with which his most benevolent deeds were repelled, and the most honest dispositions and feelings of his heart calumniated; who that calls to mind the agonies with which he was ultimately put to death, and the insulting manner in which his benevolence was recompensed; who, I say, that reflects upon all this, will feel competent to measure the height, the depth, the length, and the breadth of that love, which offered itself in sacrifice for such a people?" * "The love of Christ, which passeth knowledge," is doubly mysterious, if only a moral and not a redemptive power belongs to it. It is remedial from first to last. There is no more fitting motto for the plan of salvation than this—THE LORD OUR RIGHTENESS."

It may be well before closing this section, just to notice the way that this righteousness of Christ meets the wants of the *guilty mind.*

* Reinhard, "Plan of Christianity," p. 241.

When we analyze guilt, two distinct characteristics are seen. First, the person has a sense of *sinfulness;* secondly, he feels that he is *exposed to punishment.* Under the first experience, an *internal* work of grace is needed; under the second, an *external* work. The redemption of the God-man must be two-fold; it must be subjective and objective. *a.* The guilty man is conscious of sin; and therefore needs *pardon* and *purification.* The antecedent of pardon is *repentance;* hence the sinner must repent. When he does repent, the work of *purification* is begun. The man feels that he has broken the law, dishonored God, polluted the soul, and so he breaks off his sins by righteousness. All past sin being forgiven, and a principle of holiness introduced into the heart, the guilty conscience is quieted. In due time the person is wholly sanctified. *b.* The man is exposed to punishment; *justification* and *eternal life* are needed. The antecedent of justification is *faith;* the guilty soul must therefore believe in Christ. When the act of faith is exercised, *heaven is made sure:* "He that believeth shall be saved." The righteousness of the Redeemer enables a sinner to stand right in law when it is received by faith. The punishment that was feared is now gone forever. Peace the most serene, joy the most exulting, may possess the breast of the true Chrsitian. Sin and hell are removed; holiness and heaven are bestowed. The work of Christ thus fits exactly the sinful mind. There is a beautiful simplicity in the method of salvation when thus viewed in its relation to the constituents of guilt.

CHAPTER V.

PUNISHMENT APPREHENDED: THE DIVINE SUFFERER.

SECTION I.

THE SOUL'S PROPHECY OF FUTURE MISERY.

As we attempt to analyze this movement of the soul, we find the following points: *a.* There is a vision of a *future event.* This action of conscience is just the opposite of the action of memory. Conscience is inventive; memory is not. A thing is seen which never has happened, but which is to happen. *b.* This prophesied event belongs to *eternity*, and not to time. It is not merely future as it respects the things of earth; it is not something that will happen to one before death; but the mind crosses the grave, stands on the margin of eternity, and there beholds what is to be the lot of the wicked. *c.* The event is one of *wrath.* The prophetic announcement of the soul relates to evil, not to good; to punishment, not to reward. It is not a mere scene of affliction that the awakened mind sees before it; not a series of mighty accidents that are to befall it; but it is positive punishment. There is no sentence which expresses it with such truthfulness as this—"A fearful looking for of judgment and fiery indignation." *d.* This punishment is *objective*, both as it respects its *nature* and *author*. The mind is not the punisher: the punishment is not the same as that which conscience inflicts. The guilty soul fears another evil besides remorse; another Being besides self. Man looks forward to a Divine Judge; forward to a divine punishment.

The point, then, to be noted is this, that sinful man apprehends a *punishment different from that of conscience.* We call this punishment objective, to contradistinguish it from those subjective sufferings which are purely natural, which are the constitutional result of sin. Many have adopted a *theory* of punishment, which does not include that objective punishment we here refer to; and the reason doubtless is, that the revelations of conscience are not sufficiently examined. This we may affirm with certainty, that at the moment when one has the greatest agony of soul because of sin, he has the greatest fear of God because of that punishment which *he* is to inflict on the guilty. This shows that mere natural suffering is not deemed sufficient; it does not exhaust the full penalty of the law. As the point before us is of great importance, I propose to offer some reasons to substantiate it.

1. Men generally believe that there will be objective rewards hereafter; consequently it is equally reasonable to believe that there will be objective punishments. The idea that reward alone may be calculated on, but not punishment, is suspicious. It looks as if men were quite willing to take the good which Divine Mercy may bestow, but very unwilling to take the evil which Divine Justice deems to be necessary. If the principle be false which asserts that God will punish the wicked in addition to mental sufferings caused by sin, how can the principle be true which asserts that God will reward the righteous in addition to the mental happiness caused by holiness? The only consistent course is either to receive both or to reject both. I would have the man, then, who will not believe in the divine punishment, neither to believe in the divine reward; but to say that the only hell is a wicked heart, and

the only heaven a good one; which will give us as many hells and as many heavens as there are individuals. The man who decides against punishment is prejudiced in his own favor. The soul shrinks from suffering, while it pants for happiness. These two opposite instincts are quite likely to influence the judgment, causing it to affirm that the agreeable is alone to be looked for.

2. The general belief of the race respecting objective punishments is a strong argument in their favor. This fact is of very great importance, inasmuch as it seems to have its ground in human nature. If any one will try and muster courage enough to say that this belief of the race is not well founded, he will find it no easy matter. It is not a little remarkable to see such complete harmony, considering the fearful nature of that which is believed; and this very fact, we think, is additional proof of its correctness; for though all were to believe in future happiness as the eternal heritage of mankind, this, because of its pleasing nature, would not furnish such satisfactory evidence as the opposite fact. The few minds that have denied the doctrine of divine punishments are as nothing compared with those who have re-

ceived it; and even the denial is a presumptive proof to the contrary; for taking human nature as it is, we might by all means think that some would reject such a burning truth. Yet the whole world is wiser than any one of us.

3. If there be no objective punishments, there is no positive moral government. The very idea of a positive moral government is that of an objective system where divine authority is exercised over moral agents through the medium of law; which law has rewards and penalties affixed to it other than those that are natural. If we believe, then, that there is no punishment besides that of conscience, do we have any divine moral government? Suppose that all the penalties affixed to human laws were set aside, would there be any human government? There would not. Men might steal and kill and go to the utmost limit in wickedness, but they could not be punished, inasmuch as there is no state authority. In the same way the government of God is annihilated, if there be no positive punishment. God himself also is dethroned. Instead of being a King, he is simply a Creator; instead of being "the Judge of all the earth," he is simply the Sustainer of all the earth.

4. If there be no divine punishment, there is no accountability to God. How can God's intelligent creatures feel under obligation to obey him, since he is not their Sovereign? He cannot punish them for disobedience, be their crimes ever so aggravated. In fact, according to the theory under consideration, sin has no relation to God in any possible respect. All are sovereigns, and simply accountable to themselves. He indeed is greater than they are; but this can make no essential difference so long as he lacks power to call them to an account. All are on a level,—the Infinite and the finite stand side by side.

5. If there be no objective punishments, a premium is offered for crime. One grand idea of having a class of punishments superadded to those that are purely natural, is to restrain moral beings from sin. It is impossible, as things are, to see the highest amount of goodness, when the only penalty that is dreaded is a guilty conscience. This has great influence when united with something else; but keep it by itself, and in most cases it must fail. If any one doubts this, let him just imagine that all the governments under heaven were dissolved. What would be the result of this? The whole

world would be in a state of anarchy. The good, if there were any, would be set at naught: the wicked would riot and reign as they pleased. Tell men now that, if they commit crimes, they will feel the bad effects in a troubled conscience. What will they care for that. Such a motive is too feeble to keep the soul from rushing headlong into sin. "It is often said by Cicero and others," remarks Dr. Knapp, "that all philosophers, both Greek and Roman, are agreed in this, that the gods do not punish. But as soon as this opinion of the philosophers began to prevail among the people, it produced, according to the testimony of all Roman writers, the most disastrous consequences, which lasted for centuries. No subsequent efforts could ever succeed in awakening a fear of divine punishments in the minds of the great multitude. Hence resulted the deplorable degeneracy of the Roman empire. Truth and faith ceased, chastity became contemptible, perjury was practiced without shame, and every species of luxurious excess and of cruelty was indulged. To this corruption no philosopher was able to oppose any effectual resistance; until at length its course was arrested by Christianity." "Among Christians themselves such efforts have always been followed by similar disastrous consequences." "The papal sale of indulgences, which became general during the twelfth and succeeding centuries, and especially after the crusades, had a tendency in the same way to diminish the fear of positive divine punishments, because it was supposed one might purchase exemption from them. The result of this delusion was equally deplorable in this case as in the one before mentioned; the greatest immoralities prevailed throughout Christian lands; until this evil was arrested by the reformation, and the fear and the love of God were both awakened anew in the hearts of Christians." "A similar result took place in England in the latter half of the seventeenth century, when some rationalistic philosophers, during the reign of Charles II., undertook to emancipate the minds of men from the fear of positive divine punishments. The effect of their efforts is well known from history. Frivolity of spirit, immorality, sins of impurity, and all the dreadful consequences of forgetting God, suddenly prevailed." "The principles of these English philosophers were gradually diffused through France by the writings of Voltaire, Diderot, and others; and after 1740 they were also adopted and disseminated by some even in Germany. The history of our own times shows us sufficiently what has been the result of these principles." * Thus the demoralization consequent upon the disbelief of positive punishments is enough to show their necessity.

Reasons equally forcible with the above might be multiplied, but it is needless to enlarge. It seems obvious that there is a punishment of God, as well as a punishment of the soul. Having considered the former, we must attempt to give a brief statement of the latter. To have natural evils follow infringement of law is a wise arrangement of the Deity. If one injures his health, he will have pain; if he puts his hand into the fire, he will be burned; if he leaps from a lofty precipice, he will be killed. So, too, if one breaks the moral law, what more reasonable than to have a series of evils spring up in the soul, inflicting vengeance where it is justly due. The natural sufferings which will agitate the guilty mind in the future state may be thus analyzed:—

1. There will be complete unhappiness. This will not be occasional, but constant. And

* "Christian Theology," p. 547.

when any one considers how the soul pants for happiness, it will be seen how mighty the misery must be. There will be unceasing agony without the least alleviation. 2. There will be the conscious disapprobation of self. The soul will come down upon itself with a fearful condemnation. The light of eternity shining into the fallen spirit has made the conscience to awake; and the man abhors himself for what he is, and for what he has been. 3. There will also be the conscious disapprobation of God and the good. The soul will not dare to look up; it will shrink back into itself, the contrast will be so great. The vision of Deity, with all his spotless purity and perfect hatred of sin, will be enough to isolate the soul forever. The never-dying spirit will be utterly petrified in its dark and deep depravity. It cannot look the Divine One in the face; and despising itself, it does this the more by reason of the eternal frown of the Supreme. The wicked soul will feel also in the keenest manner the disapprobation of all the good. There will be the intense realization that every pure being condemns, and must condemn. Thus the soul will be unable to gain the least respect from any whose respect is desirable. Condemned by self, by God, by all the good, the soul can only harrow itself on this account. 4. Shame therefore will take possession of the sinful mind. It can gain the favor of none; it is disgraced, held in contempt; and so it stands abashed and confounded; conscious of its fallen condition the more by reason of the purity and opinions of others. The soul will see what it might have been; how holy and happy; the associate of the noble and good; but now the companion of the most depraved. This fact realized will drink up the very life of the spirit. 5. Bitter sorrow will then take pessession of the soul. Grief, such as this world never saw, will wring the spirit from hour to hour, as it evermore sees and feels its outcast and abandoned condition. The fountain of sorrow in the soul will be tumultuous with a new energy, and it will flow through all the parts thereof. One sea of mental anguish will ever heave; and there will be nothing but "weeping and wailing and gnashing of teeth." 6. Passions will rage among themselves, will seek to be satisfied, but will not. A thousand wants will cry: they will not be regarded. There will be a continual craving from different points of the soul: nothing shall feed the eternal hunger.

Consequently the immortal spirit will devour itself. 7. Remorse will be kindled into a burning intensity by the lamp of memory. The past will crowd about the soul; and it will writhe and groan and suffer and die. Remorse will sit upon the heart and gnaw it like a vulture, will sting it like a fiery serpent; and this shall be continuous as the hours, and endless as the night of hell. 8. Black despair will then settle down upon the soul. No good will appear within the whole compass of mind; nothing but evil, nothing but misery,—hope will be dead. Night without a single ray; gloomy, sullen, dreary. The soul will be hemmed in. Though surrounded with millions, there will be a profound solitude. What a sight in eternity to see a soul exiled within itself!—a soul alone in absolute agony and despair!—scorched and withered and dead!

Such, in condensed language, is a statement of the natural consequences of sin; that punishment which the soul will inflict on itself. What we say it is, is as nothing to what it shall be. Suffering endured, is far different from suffering delineated. Is this, however, the whole of natural punishment? Is it correct to confine it to the simple action of the mind? Will there be no suffering connected with the *future body?* However common it may be to confine natural punishment to the soul, I must believe that the body will share in the misery of hereafter. The material part of man suffers in the present life on account of moral evil, and why should it not suffer in the future life? I admit that the body which the soul is to inhabit throughout eternity will be, in many respects, different from that which now lives and dies. It will doubtless have greater capabilities and powers. But this very fact rather increases than lessens the evil. If the future body be so made that, when allied to a pure mind, its enjoyment is increased a thousand-fold, then, when allied to an impure mind, its misery is increased to the same extent. The greater the being, the greater the joy or sorrow. Fulness of created life, intense vigor, eagerness to expatiate in a boundless sphere, yet no opportunity to exercise,—this would necessarily produce extreme agony. The whole material nature would thus be turned into one raging appetite, eternally craving, but eternally unheeded. "If corporeal restraint and imprisonment be one of the most intolerable of bodily ills, what shall imprisonment be when the locomotive energy is a thousand times more vehement than at present, and when the exercise of it is attended with no conscious effort, and is followed by no lassitude, and when the widest and the fairest fields shall lie in prospect before it? The chain of the captive is galling, in proportion, or nearly so, to the captive's animal vigor and elastic spirit. Let it then be imagined that the future man, new born to his inheritance of absolute mechanical force—the inherent force of mind, and finding himself able at will to traverse all spaces, should, in the very hour wherein he he has made proof of his recent faculty, be stopped, either by malignant superior powers, or by the dread ministers of justice, and on account of forgotten misdeeds, be seized, enchained, incarcerated!"* By this simple thought, it can be seen how much of suffering may be connected with the state or condition of the body.

When it is understood also that the mind hereafter will be aroused to unwonted energy, we can easily perceive how its intensified thought, its unutterable grief, its raging sin, will wound and poison and torment the body.

* Isaac Taylor, "Physical Theory of another Life," chap. x.

It is impossible for the one nature to be affected and not the other. "We must never forget," says Dr. Channing, "that in that world mind or character is to exert an all-powerful sway; and accordingly, it is rational to believe, that the corrupt and deformed mind, which wants moral goodness, or a spirit of concord with God and with the universe, will create for itself, as its fit dwelling, a deformed body, which will also want concord or harmony with all things around it. Suppose this to exist, and the whole creation which now amuses, may become an instrument of suffering, fixing the soul with a more harrowing consciousness on itself. You know that even now, in consequence of certain derangements of the nervous system, the beautiful light gives acute pain, and sounds, which once delighted us, become shrill and distressing. How often this excessive irritableness of the body has its origin in moral disorders, perhaps few of us suspect. I apprehend, indeed, that we should be all amazed, were we to learn to what extent the body is continually incapacitated for enjoyment, and made susceptible of suffering, by sins of the heart and life." How easily, then, may the mind hereafter frame the future body according to itself, so that, in proportion to its vice, it will receive, through its organs and senses, impressions of gloom, which it will feel to be the natural productions of its own depravity." *

SECTION II.

THE GOD-MAN A SUFFERER.

The doctrine of the innocent suffering for the guilty is oftentimes presented under an array of defensive argument that appears to us wholly unnecessary. It looks as if we were clinging to some abstract speculation pertaining to the divine government,----a speculation which runs counter to the immutable rectitude and justice of the Deity. As well discuss the question whether a finite intelligence can sin under the administration of a God of absolute love, as whether a sinless person can suffer under the administration of a God of absolute justice. Both are *facts;* and that ends the matter. Man has fallen: Christ has died. The sceptic, not less than the Christian, believes that Jesus suffered. The only difference

* Works, vol. iv. p. 164, Boston ed.

between the two is—the former asserts that he suffered for no sins at all; the latter, that he laid down his life for the guilty. Which view harmonizes with truth and right can only be seen by attending carefully to the sublime fact itself. Which view furnishes a full and adequate reason for the sufferings of Jesus will appear from what follows.

The fact that eighteen hundred years ago an innocent person suffered ought to arrest attention. Why should it be? The mind is really startled. A strange thing has happened in the universe. It is true, in a certain sense, that the innocent oftentimes suffer in this world *on account* of the guilty, though not *in the room and stead* of the guilty. Children suffer *because* of wicked parents, citizens *because* of wicked rulers. Such kind of vicarious suffering is, indeed, common under the present constitution of things. Yet it is worthy of special attention that all who thus suffer are not *sinless*, but *sinful*. Even infants belong to a depraved race. There is a disease in all souls; a shadow covers them; death reigns. The resemblance is not complete therefore between the so-called innocents of earth, and the Innocent One of heaven. He is the solitary Sufferer of humanity. "He trod the wine-press alone; and of the people there was none with him." As far as we know, but one pure and holy being has suffered in the government of God. This may well astonish us. When Christ made known to his disciples that he should "suffer many things of the elders and chief priests and scribes, and be killed," I am not surprised that "Peter took him, and began to rebuke him, saying, Be it far from thee Lord: this shall not be unto thee." Clearly enough this is the first impulse of mind awakened by the sight of stainless purity. Why should the innocent thus suffer and die? No trifling reason will account for this. The isolation and strangeness of the whole affair point to some great and comprehensive plan; some mighty emergency is to be met, some lofty purpose to be realized.

And yet I am told that Jesus suffered that he might show an *example* to the race! Really this appears like irony. The thought is presented in its most favorable light by Dr. Channing. "We are to visit the cross," he says, "not to indulge a natural softness, but to acquire firmness of spirit, to fortify our minds for hardship and suffering in the cause of duty and of human happiness. To live as Christ lived, to die as Christ died, to give up ourselves as sacrifices to God, to conscience, to whatever good interest we can advance,—these are the lessons written with the blood of Jesus. His cross is to inspire us with a calm courage, resolution, and superiority to all temptation." * These are noble lessons that are to be taught by the crucifixion of "the Lord of glory." But surely, if such be the explanation of suffering innocence, the whole is shrouded in the most profound mystery. Wonderful example truly, that the most perfect life should have connected with it the most extreme anguish and pain! Does the Sovereign of the universe mean to teach me that the greater my sin, the less my punishment? the greater my holiness, the more abundant my suffering? Whatever example the patient Redeemer may have shown me by his sorrowful life and painful death, I cannot but think that an example of a different kind is exhibited to mortals by the Divine Being himself, which really destroys any good impression that might be made on the souls of men by Calvary and the cross. The manifest want of wisdom and justice on the part of the

* Works, vol. iv, p. 207.

Deity by this view of the matter is so apparent that we cannot for a moment receive it. The light that seems to come to man darkens the Godhead. A needless sacrifice is made. Why such agony and woe, merely to teach me the superior virtues of human nature?----virtues which are admitted to have made their appearance long before the Messianic age. If I desire to see noble trust and faithfulness, they are found in Abraham; if rectitude and patience, in Job; if fortitude and self-denial, in the martyred prophets. I say not that the best and greatest of men were equal to Jesus, for they were imperfect while he was perfect, they were human while he was divine; but I do say that the lesson which he was supposed to teach by his collective sufferings could have been taught at a less price, and with less injury to the moral system of God.

And what increases the difficulty is that I behold an *unusual depth* and *keenness* to the sufferings of Christ. It is not that he pressed forward to illustrate the whole of a perfected morality with pain and punishment before him, but it is that his soul was evermore agitated with the deepest grief that makes his case peculiar. There was an agony of mind apart from, and independent of, all the persecutions of the wicked. A mysterious sorrow possessed his spirit, which cannot be explained upon natural principles. He was perfectly holy—why then this sorrow? Admit that he suffered at the hands of men, this does not account for the peculiar fact. Just before his betrayal, he is the subject of the most painful emotions. He says, "My soul is exceedingly sorrowful, even unto death." Three times he offers up the same condensed prayer of grief: "O my Father, if it be possible, let this cup pass from me." What does this mean? Hundreds of men have gone to the stake rejoicing,—men who were guilty and needed forgiveness; yet the only innocent being that has appeared since the Adamic fall is in trouble,—trouble, if we may believe it, such as others passed through with the greatest ease! He even craves the sympathy of his three favored disciples: "tarry ye here, and watch with me." The infinite Redeemer begs support from his creatures! "He, the helper of the world, confesses to those to whom he brings help his own need of it, and really requests help from those even who were unable to render it." The rationalistic hypothesis is not sufficient to explain this. The Biblical view is the only true one: "He was wounded for our transgressions, he was bruised for our iniquities." I make no attempts to measure his agony; I say not that he suffered the concentrated punishment of the misery everlasting; I only affirm that his suffering was unique, was great; that it has had no parallel in time. I can see as he hung on the cross, that he had other sufferings than those that were the result of crucifixion; other than those that were produced by priest and scribe with all their hatred; other than those that the two thieves on either side of him experienced,—sufferings which no martyr or criminal at the scaffold ever knew. What is the theological import of that strange cry, "My God, my God, why hast thou forsaken me?" The mind is confused and puzzled if we admit no atonement in all this. To say that he suffered as an example is without fitness or reason. No idea but that of a world's redemption is the one that explains the matter. There is no possible reason why God should forsake his Son, leaving him in darkness, dismay, and agony of soul, upon the supposition that he was merely showing to mankind the noblest of the active and passive virtues. We should rather think that the most blessed revelations of the Divine Being would have illumined and comforted his mind at the trying moment. Yea, it is matter of *certainty* that God must have acted in this manner, inasmuch as Christ was a sinless being. There seems therefore, a complete turning round of the moral attributes of the Deity by such strange conduct. An eclipse covers the mind of Jesus and the mind of God at the same instant of time, when both, according to the hypothesis, ought to have been luminous with visible joy. The divine benevolence is thus at fault. The moral reason of man affirms that God will smile upon the good and will frown upon the evil, but here he seems to do the contrary. I can understand all this, when I know that the God-man took the place of the guilty and suffered for them; but by the opposite view there is nothing but confusion. The whole matter comes to this, that Christ either was a sinner, or he made an atonement. If he sinned, his sufferings were the result of his own guilt: if he was sinless, his sufferings were endured for the guilt of others. That he was without sin is the common belief; consequently he suffered and died for sinners of mankind.

Now, the singularity and greatness of the

passion of Jesus fit exactly the troubled conscience of man. Guilt cries out for suffering; and the more intense the suffering the more satisfaction there is to the moral faculty. If God has to be appeased, so has man. The human nature is fashioned according to the image of the divine nature. The wrath of conscience has the same meaning as the wrath of God. That is, there is a recoil from moral evil, there is an abhorance of it, there is indignation against it, there is a cry for punishment, in both cases. When I see a criminal so tormented in his mind that he must deliver himself up to be punished, in order to satisfy his conscience, I can see at a glance the moral fitness of the sufferings of Christ. Salvation without suffering is impossible. All the painful rites of Heathenism prove it. All the forebodings of the guilty establish it. What is the moral significance of the suicide of Judas? Obviously this, that he considered his sin too great for forgiveness or atonement. He slew himself as if he would present a human sacrifice to satisfy the burning anger of his soul. The body was put to death: the soul was committed over to God to be punished. This might be called a natural atonement. It was the climax of human power in the line of making a sacrifice for sin,—more cannot be done than this. Guilt may make one slay a lamb, a child; but when it compels to self-immolation, the end is reached. It is strange that this last and greatest of human atonements should stand side by side with the divine atonement,—the natural and the supernatural were together. The despair and death of man introduced hope and life from God. Yea, the very sin which occasioned the destruction of Judas, occasioned the crucifixion of Jesus! Never were guilt and suffering so strangely connected.

Then, too, we ought to know that although conscience apprehends a *punishment* that is *future*, the punishment is grounded upon a *sin* that is *past;* and, consequently, the sufferings of the God-man must be retrospective in their influence. The true idea ef the atonement is shadowed forth in this strange action of the mind. My fear of the divine punishment is proportioned to the amount of my past transgression; hence the sufferings of Christ have a bearing on the punishment just to the extent that they have a bearing on the sin that causes it. They could not relate to one, to the exclusion of the other. The atonement, therefore, is but the outward expression of the inward experience. The cross and the conscience fit each other. This being the case, what effect does the death of Jesus have upon the *punishment* of man?

1. The greater part of punishment is held back from every human being during the present life. It is certain that the full penalty of the law is not executed upon any one of the human family during his sojourn in time; and the only way of accounting for this is by the atonement of the Redeemer. He who was innocent suffered: we who are guilty do not suffer. Why this strange state of things in the government of a holy and just God? It seems that the divine justice must be satisfied by the death of the God-man, and that on this account a merciful economy has been introduced. It is clear that we do not live under a strictly legal administration, for that knows nothing of a suspension of punishment. When superior beings sinned in heaven, they were instantly cast down to hell. Why, then, should the human race be permitted to remain upon earth? In no other way can this be answered but upon the principle that a redemptive dynasty is now in existence. Indeed, all man-

kind have acted upon this supposition; for they have prayed and worshipped, lived and died, with thoughts of forgiveness and reformation as among the possibilities of time. It is true that the whole of punishment is not removed from the present scene of being, inasmuch as that is morally impossible. As man sins he must suffer; hence we have natural punishment. But yet it is manifest that subjective evils are not felt to that extent that they will be hereafter,—even *they* are limited. As to objective punishment, that is but feebly manifested under the present system of grace. Nations are under a law of retribution which completes itself in time, as they cannot exist in their collective capacity in eternity; individuals as such are punished in the future. The race, too, viewed as one whole, suffers on account of the primal fall: "In Adam all die." The sufferings of Christ do not set aside temporal death. Enough that they hold it in abeyance for a limited period, that man may have time for spiritual culture.

2. Faith in a suffering Saviour cancels future and eternal punishment. Here is found the most significant characteristic of the atonement. When a man is justified, heaven is cer-

tain. He may have doubts and fears, yet according to the divine method of grace all is safe hereafter. Justification by grace is as firm and sure as justification by law. If possible, it is more firm and more sure, because he who redeems from the curse of the law has in store a vast surplus of merit after the salvation of countless millions. It would seem also that if one is saved from eternal misery, he is no less saved from *eternal sin;* yet the latter thought is seldom mentioned. If redeemed from the one evil, why not from the other? Man saved has not experienced any of the future punishment, neither has he experienced any of the future sin; hence his relation to both is the same, and his deliverance from the one is not more complete and joyful than his deliverance from the other. In fact, sin is the evil of evils: redemption from its power is the greatest of blessings.

3. What is the bearing of the death of the Son of God on the trial and punishment of the wicked? As Christ raises all from their graves, so he is the Judge of all. It is proper that the present administration should be closed up by the Mediator, as without him it could have had no existence. It is generally supposed

that a final judgment is for the purpose of manifesting the justice of God. However true this may be, it does not let us into the full secret of the matter. There is a reason, I think, found in the very nature of a moral government for a public trial and sentence. If the government of God were *natural,* and *not positive,* there would be no place for a day of reckoning, inasmuch as sentence and punishment generally move along with the commission of sin. Those persons are consistent who, disbelieving a positive government, reject a judgment to come; for the two go together. If there be a scheme of things additional and external to that which is found in the natural working of mind, then, most assuredly there must be a trial additional and external to that which is found in the court of conscience. The apparatus of the divine moral government would not be complete without this. The gathering together of the fallen angels is another proof that a day of reckoning is a necessity of government. Their first sentence was not enough; they must appear in company with all the generations of time, and in public trial before the universe of God be condemned. Moral government has a grandeur and sublimity connected with it, as well as a fixedness and security, when thus seen carrying out its demands before the whole kingdom of mind.

With the scenes of the judgment, the present system ends. The wicked go to their own place. The death of Christ sends out no saving influence among the companies of the lost. Punishment never can change the character of souls. We do not say to the abandoned that if they will not cease sinning, we shall see to it that they are made saints in perdition. If redemption fails of saving men here, it is not reasonable to suppose that punishment will save them hereafter. If punishment could be thus effectual, it would have a preëminence over redemption, making the latter to be superfluous. It is certainly not a a small mistake to have a system of salvation inferior to a system of punishment. God must have made a blunder when he selected the Christian remedy; for those who are too wicked to be purified by it are yet purified by punishment. Even Judas is after all perfected! Yea, he who has committed the unpardonable sin is saved! Why was not hell established in this world instead of salvation, that all might be made holy before death?—thus causing less suffering. Indeed, some have really adopted this view. Man is punished here for his sins, and all are saved. This is consistent. But those, who are not willing to go so far as this, say that it is not by punishment alone that the soul is to be purified in the future world,—salvation is used with it. If this is so, the two are together here; for we have the same kind of punishment in this world that will be in the next according to the opinion of such persons, viz., a *guilty conscience*, they not believing in what is called positive punishment. If salvation and natural punishment, then, cannot save some hardened sinners here, we do not see how the same means can save them hereafter, especially as they have been growing worse and worse during the whole of their stay upon earth. To all who are so certain touching the ultimate restoration of the wicked, I commend the following passage taken from the works of Dr. Channing; for it seems that that great man was not quite sure of the matter, as the closing words plainly show. He remarks: "One and only one evil can be carried from this world to the next, and that is, the evil within us, moral evil, guilt, crime, ungoverned passion, the depraved mind, the memory of a wasted or ill-spent life, the character which has grown up under neglect of God's voice in the soul and in his word. This, this will go with us, to stamp itself on our future frames, to darken our future being, to separate us like an impassable gulf from our Creator, and from pure and happy beings, to be as a consuming fire and an undying worm." "I have spoken of the pains and penalties of moral evil, or of wrong doing, in the world to come. How long they will endure, I know not. Whether they will issue in the reformation and happiness of the sufferer, or will terminate in the extinction of his conscious being, is a question on which Scripture throws no clear light." * *There is not a single instance on record of a man's repenting in perdition.*

At the end of the redemptive kingdom, a new dynasty begins in eternity. If it is true that the righteous are to go away into eternal life, it is equally true that the wicked are to go away into eternal punishment. If the one class are to be forever saved, the other class are to be forever lost. If the bad may reach heaven, the good may reach hell. The time is coming in the onward movements of the divine government when all the wicked of the universe

* Works, vol. iv. p. 166.

are to be removed to a solitary world by themselves. The evil are to mingle no more with the good. As if all the criminals of earth were confined on some island of the deep, the great remaining population being perfectly holy, so in the system of God all transgressors are to be banished into eternal exile, never more to break in upon the quiet and harmony of sanctified minds. One dark world is to career forever. No Sun is ever to arise upon its night. Its people few, compared with the infinite numbers of the universe, they are never to increase or decrease while God endures. They are imprisoned for life,—the life of eternity.

CHAPTER VI.

HUMAN SORROW: THE DIVINE SYMPATHIZER.

SECTION I.

THE VOICE OF SORROW.

No fact is truer than sorrow, for it is a fact of the heart. The moment one speaks of it, the soul bears witness of its reality. The chapter of every man's life has in it many pages of grief. The biography of a human spirit has to be written in part with tears. "The uncertain tenure of our happiness presses upon an ever-present anxiety, and we vainly strive to fortify ourselves against those multiform chances that threaten us on every side. No sooner does a benediction fall upon our fireside than we begin to think of its easy departure. Our sabbaths, hallowed on high, bring a short interlude of peace between the toils of a setting and a rising sun, and our gladdest songs are mellowed by a sadness that the spirit knows too well must be its abiding portion. Such themes, indeed, occur in all literature that relates to human experience; but there are various methods of treating them. As mere histories, they abound in novels and tragedies; but how few ever penetrate their import and draw from them the essential grandeur of their instructions! How rare to find their divine language translated into the words that circulate among mortals! Over the birth of sorrow who have watched? And who can tell its mysterious agency as it travels abroad with the everlasting night, and wraps its strange texture of sackcloth around its myriad subjects? And who can read the hidden meaning of those tears that fall around the altars of our solitude, and exhale to heaven without a witnessing eye? Alas for the sanctity of sorrow! Men have paraded it upon the stage to play a part, to answer an end, to relieve gaiety. Others have used it as a shallow thing, and dismissed it as a fugitive trifle. Some have reverenced it; but the worship was in the outer court, and the real sanctuary heard not their uprising strain."

The most profound conception of human sorrow is that it belongs to the *higher nature* of man. Many seem to be unconscious of any other sorrow than that which is connected with our sympathetic nature. In the afflictions of life, especially in the loss of friends, this kind of sorrow appears. One cord after another is snapped asunder, and the soul is in trouble. But the darkest and deepest sorrow is back of this; it is found in the agony of a sick and dying spirit. The mere natural sympathies show that man is human, the supernatural sympathies show that he is divine. The latter being cut loose from God, the exiled spirit sighs and laments in its dreary orphanage. It is the sorrow of this higher region that many never reach. They look only on the outside; they see the drops falling from the leaves of the tree shaken by the wind; they think that that is all. It is the soul-sorrow which all should comprehend; that which is found in man's imperial nature all in ruins. It is the native sighing of the crushed spirit, as the stones and rubbish lie heavily upon it. Not till this more profound grief of the God-nature of the soul is realized will sorrow be thoroughly understood. It is when one wakes up to a clear consciousness of this deep inward lamentation that he realizes there must be something radically wrong at the fountain-head of being. He sees that the little springs among the hills are poisoned; that a malady exists at the very root of life. There is a weeping choir ever hymning forth their sad song in the deep subteranean chambers of the spirit, like a company of funeral angels playing on their harps in the rocky sepulchre at the still hour of night.

Sorrow is generally associated in our minds with poverty, disappointment, sickness, death; but these are rather the occasions than the causes of it. At the most, these are the cold currents which, sweeping across, distil the vapors of the sky, and make the showers descend. The philosophy of sorrow and the philosophy of sin are intimately connected. As the eagle pierced with the arrow and brought to the earth ever seeks to rise again, but cannot, so is it with man. He was made to dwell on high; but being sorely wounded by the archers, he takes up his abode in the valley of life, in the midst of solitude and sorrow. It is quite clear that grief is the native language of the soul. I have even seen the little infant sigh when no scar seemed upon its angel spirit; and in its sleep, though a seraph watched beside it, it has had its deep breathing of sadness. It would seem as if the flower was crushed while just opening its leaves to the sun. The old pilgrim leaning upon his staff and the little child on the bosom of its mother, have each a tear to let fall, and a heart-pang which opens the fountains of grief. Doubtless there is a smile, too, which makes the countenance look glad, even as the light of a candle a dark room; yet the gladness is only like the bubbles which gather on the top of the stream that speedily burst, and are no more.

It is a very great mistake to suppose that *outward good* expels sorrow from the heart. Perfect circumstances cannot make a man happy. Health and gold never can bid away grief from the soul. The sick and the poor are not the only sufferers. Joy and sorrow are not confined to classes. Neither the princely man nor the sage is free from the spirit's woe. No outward adorning however regnant and glorious can avail. The king on his throne, with crowds of worshippers before him, may look as if sorrow never laid her cold hand on his heart; yet the monarch sighs in the midst of the adulations of the multitude; the diadem begirts a brow wrinkled with care. The most smiling countenance has back of it a cloud;

the most sparkling eye tells not all the truth. "Even in laughter the heart is sorrowful; and the end of that mirth is heaviness." I have seen the gay youth and the man ride their round of pleasure, yet in the midst of it all there was a thorn in the soul; for when the pleasure had ceased, the pain that was there before was now felt the more keenly. Sorrow inhabits the night-land of the soul. Tears are its symbol; weeping is its speech; lamentation is its echo. Sorrow is not the mere turmoil which one sees on the surface of the lake, caused by the force of the passing wind; but it is the deep under-current, dark and sluggish in its course.

There is a *loneliness* that characterizes sorrowful minds, which deserves a moment's notice. Persons who are pressed down with a burden of grief shut themselves up in a world of their own into which no stranger is allowed to enter. The soul loves to commune and sigh alone, with never a witnessing eye or ear to take knowledge of the sacred scene. More especially is this true when the fountain of tears is dried up. Then the soul sits solitary, and thinks over its affliction. That sorrow is the deepest which has few tears. He who weeps much has but a surface sorrow. All rude minds are loud in their lamentation, and quick in their joy. The refined nature is ever subdued in its grief, and silent oftentimes in the midst of its greatest agony. It is a mistake to think that he who weeps but seldom is of a hard heart; there are other channels besides those that are seen. We know there are some who deem it beneath them to let fall a tear; but these are not men. There are others who are ever crying about trifles, with whom we have no sympathy. There is a sanctity about sorrow which we would not have defiled by constant weeping. A child will often cry for what it cannot have; but this betokens self-will rather than sorrow. So many a one when crossed in his ways will shed tears, which are but drops from the cloud of wrath. Secret, silent grief is the most natural. Who has not felt when approaching one deeply affected with sorrow that not a word could be spoken to him; the very sight of the person intimated that it is best to say nothing. Before such a presence there is only a solemn silence; there is a feeling speaking in the countenance, but no more. The conduct of the men who came to comfort Job in his distress is true to the life: "They sat down with him upon the ground seven days and seven nights, and none spake a word unto him : for they saw that his grief was very great." Yes, there is a groaning of spirit which cannot be uttered. All feeling when deepest is too spiritual for words. It is not strange, then, that one should erect his tent on the borders of the evening-land, and there alone commune with the sighs of the soul, the weeping prayers of the heart.

But here we are reminded of what may be called *unconscious* sorrow. To a heart habituated to grief, as to one habituated to anything else, there is oftentimes no consciousness of the sad condition of the soul. This is most strikingly seen in children who are really affected with sadness. Sometimes they are so circumstanced in life that they naturally grow up in the midst of sorrow without knowing it. Their souls bleed many a time on account of the multiplied evils which beset the poor and the vicious with whom they are connected by the ties of nature. There is something peculiarly affecting in beholding a little child with a pale, sad countenance. It is unnatural; for we expect to see joy and hope sparkling in the eye and smiling in the face of the young. A shadow darkens the soul; and what excites our sympathy the most is the strange fact of apparent unconsciousness. We see one suffering without being aware of it. There are weights pressing upon the little heart, yet all seems natural to the child. No other lot has ever been experienced, and so no change seems to be longed for.

A very touching case, which occurred in one of our large cities, we will mention, as it illustrates the thought before us in the most tender manner. There were three children (the oldest of whom was only eight years of age) at the station-house along with their mother, who was dead beside them. The eldest child, a girl, was examined by the Coroner in regard to the circumstances of her mother's death. Her story is so simple and artless that one is tenderly impressed by it. Pointing to the corpse, she said: "That is my mother. The night before last, two men came into our house, and turned my father and mother and me and my two little brothers out. We had no where to go. We then went to sleep in an entry. Nobody turned us away all night. In the morning father went away to look for another place. He was gone all day. We had nothing to eat, and were very hungry. Father came back at six o'clock, and then went away again. Nobody would let us into their house, because they said, if they did, the landlord would turn them out. The folks we hired the house of hired it of somebody else. So we went into the yard. Mother said she was very sick; she had been sick a long time before, and my little brothers cried. Mother lay down, and I put some rags on her to keep her warm, because, she said, her head ached so bad. When it got dark, my two little brothers lay down, and I put some things over them, and I got some rags to put under them too; and then I sat up to watch. By and by a policeman came along, and then he went away and got another one, and they lifted mother up and put her into a cart and brought us all here." How exceedingly touching is a scene like this! How much of unconscious sorrow was locked up in the soul of that little girl! Her care for her two younger brothers, who also were sad and knew it not, and for her mother, who died a few hours after she was taken away, shows what we mean better than we can describe it. During the whole continuance of her ministry of love, she seemed not to know the sorrow that had given a character and cast to her whole being.

There is another peculiar characteristic of sorrow, viz., its affinity for *soft sounds*. How natural to speak to one in trouble in a low tone of voice. We do this almost instinctively. If having entered a house, we are speaking loudly, not knowing that any sorrowful one is present, the voice is changed the instant the discovery is made. If we are visiting a sick and dying man, we find ourselves talking in subdued accents. This is not done because noise would disturb the invalid, for after he is dead, the same soft manner is continued. Just enter the dwelling at the time of the funeral, and you will find individuals speaking almost in a whisper. Music, too, of a plaintive character is selected, as that falls gently and softly on the ear. It seems thus to soothe the heavy heart. It is very curious also that the sense of *hearing* comes nearer to the *heart* than the sense of sight. The eye is intellectual: the ear is emotional. "Next to sight," remarks Sir William Hamilton, "hearing affords us, in the shortest interval, the greatest variety and multitude of cognitions; and as sight divides space almost to infinity, through color, so hearing does the same to time, through sound. Hearing is, however, much less extensive in its sphere of knowledge or perception than sight; but in the same proportion is its capacity of feeling or sensation more intensive. We have greater pleasure and greater pain from single sounds than from single colors; and, in like manner concords and discords, in the one sense, affect us more agreeably or disagreeably, than any modifications of light in the other." * The human voice has always been the most powerful to win the heart. Words read will make quite a different impression from the same words heard. The blind generally have much feeling. They are children of the heart, for their chief sense is the ear. They love music. The deaf are less emotional. They are apt to be suspicious, which dries up the life of the feelings. It can thus be seen that there is a philosophical connection between sound and sorrow. The sweet echoes of sympathy falling on the ear like the words of angels, close up the wounds of the broken heart, and pour balm thereon like to that which distills from the trees of God.

And what is quite peculiar, there is *joy* connected with sorrow. This may seem a paradox to some, yet it is certainly a significant truth.

* "Metaphysics," p. 336.

It is well known that all men love to *feel*. And the great majority of men love that kind of public speaking which makes them feel; yea, more, they eagerly covet that which makes them *weep*. What multitudes rush to the theatre when certain plays are to be performed, —plays which will excite the tender feelings. These are spoken of afterwards with the greatest interest; and no ground of praise is thought more reasonable than this—that the audience could not keep from shedding tears during the performance. How eagerly, too, those kind of books are read which influence the mind in the same way. Such works are among the most popular that we have. One will read and read, though he can scarcely see through his tears. He will wipe his eyes, and begin again with a most pleasant perseverance. It would seem as if the Creator had arranged the human constitution so as to mitigate the evils of sorrow as far as he possibly could. The dark cloud is either fringed with gold, or arched by a rainbow. The desert has a well; the carcass of a lion, honey.

Here is a group of children going to plant flowers by a mother's grave. They are both sad and joyful. They reach the place of the dead. They dig gently round the grave of their mother. They almost think that she is asleep, and would not wake her. Gladly would they see her face; gladly would they hear her words. While planting the different flowers, they mention how she felt and looked when she died. The younger children join in the conversation, and ask when their mother will come back again. The elder reply that she has gone to heaven, and they will never see her more; but they must be good, and when they die they will go and dwell with her forever. Now the work of love is finished, and they feel happy that in a little while the flowers will bloom sweetly. They will evermore return again, and sit down beside them and watch them as they grow. "Here is the little grave where sister is buried. Do you remember when we used to play among the trees on the summer's day? But she took sick and died; and mother said she is now an angel, and would never be sick or die again." They all now return to their home; and while the younger have a kind of indistinct sadness and a more distinct joy, the older have a clearer apprehension of sorrow and a quieter kind of happiness; yet both blending together constitute two of the beautiful realities of life. Joy is all the more attractive in that it rises out of the tumultuous sea of sorrow.

But we must not forget that sorrow is a means of *discipline.* It is one of the great thoughts of the Eternal Mind, evolved in the development of humanity, that evil becomes the occasion of good. Viewing man as he is, he could never arrive at such a high state of perfection without sorrow as with it. There must be a remedy proportioned to the nature of the disease. That which is pleasant is not always the best fitted to remove that which is unpleasant. The cure and the complaint are in some sense alike. The very evils that are the result of sin become to the good man the means of improvement. He who has not realized this truth practically has never yet entered into the deep philosophy of suffering. That man is the wisest who makes everything the means of moral discipline. To him who seeks to be transformed into the image of God, everything works together for his good. We only speak in this way of sinful man, and not of those celestial intelligences who have never wandered from their Maker. It is not to be supposed that the whole realm of mind is to be educated by sorrow and pain. But for man in process of restoration, the evils that beset him on every side are perfectly adapted to accomplish the end. He who battles his way to glory and honor on high will be a stronger man forever, than if he had found his way thither without foe or frown. In this way at least, we have a practical solution of the mysterious problem of evil. The higher and more transcendental solution we cannot reach; God alone understands that as it is. It is pleasant at any rate to know that the better spirits of time shall one day stand erect in the purity of manhood, when the afflictions of the present economy shall be needed no more. While here, they may not forget that higher conception of a divine philosophy that man is made perfect through suffering. "Those wish not wisely who desire life to be like one strain of music, or the sparkle of a summer's wave. Suffering often calls forth our best feelings and the highest energies of the mind. It exalts and purifies. It awakens a true spirit, and naturally leads us nearer heaven. As the shadow of Peter is said to have given life to those upon whom it rested, so often will sorrow give higher life to the soul." The night of weeping loses itself in the morning of joy. Life is a great antithesis. The evil and the good, the human and the divine, are ever at work. The perfection of man will be at the end of storms.

There appears almost to be something divine about sorrow, though nothing is more human. The greatest minds bend under its power. "Whatever is highest and holiest is tinged with melancholy. The eye of genius has always a plaintive expression, and its natural language is pathos. A prophet is sadder than other men; and he who was greater than all prophets was 'a man of sorrows, and acquainted with grief.'"

SECTION II.

THE GOD-MAN A SYMPATHIZER.

THE sympathy of Christ was of the purest texture because of a certain *delicacy* of soul and character which he possessed. There was an extremely fine finish to his whole being and benevolence. No rough points were found in his composition. His nature was a complete circle. He was harmony. The whole movement of his being was just as it should be.

He never went too far, never did too little, on all occasions he was perfection.

There is what may be called an *inviting quality* in the sympathy of the Son of God. It would have all men to bring their sorrows and troubles to him, that thus they might find relief and rest. By this lovely trait Christ shows himself to be the heart-friend of man. There is no anguish so deep, no affliction so painful, that need hinder the soul from coming to him. The heavier the burden, the greater the need of help. Every soul knows that it has a trouble which it can tell into the ear of no mortal man; there being a consciousness that no mere earthly creature can measure or meet our grief. Hence we bear it about with us wherever we go. To the friend that is nearest to us we make it not known. The child says nothing to the parent, neither does the parent say anything to the child. The husband is silent in the presence of his wife, and the wife is equally silent in the presence of her husband. But we have found the one Comforter of men to whom the soul may be opened. There is no want or woe but that he can meet, no sigh or sin but that he can take away. He bears our griefs, he carries our sorrows; and the more completely we cast our troubles upon him, the more completely does he pour into the soul joy and peace.

As it respects sympathy, there is much in the fact that Christ was a *man*. The soul needs to be drawn "with the cords of a man, with bands of love." Christ may be spoken of as *the* man,—the one human being complete in every sense of that word, leaving no part of the ideal unrealized. There is one thought which we must not miss—the thought that he *grew up* into manhood, that he was a *fully developed* man. In this particular he differed from Adam. Adam had no infancy or childhood; no youth even. He had no past to which he might look back. He was a man from the start. Christ had a past; and he reached manhood by degrees. Yet, though Jesus passed through the periods of infancy and youth, we think of him chiefly as the man. Indeed, the fact that the early part of his life is almost shrouded from our view is an intimation that we should look to him mainly in the public manhood of his existence. If we thus fix the eye upon Christ as the developed man, he is seen as the very being who can meet our wants. The Christ of Palestine is the Christ of the world. Jesus living among the men of Canaan and blessing them is a typical representation of what he is to do for the race till time shall end. Subtracting the miracles of Christ, what remains is a prophecy of the unfolding of redemption. The Jews were types of all mankind; and the mission of Christ was typical of the whole redemptive work. We have reason, then, to think that if Christ sympathized with men while he was upon earth, he will now sympathize with them while he is in heaven. Important meaning is attached in this way to the *life* of the Redeemer. Christ must die. That is a settled point in God's administration of mercy. But is it saying too much that he must also live? If the death of Christ were all, why did he live so many years? Why did he not die at the age of twenty or twelve, instead of at the age of thirty-three? The point is clear that manhood was to be reached. Through time and through eternity he is to be the Man of men.

It is doubtful, however, whether we can reach the whole of the idea under the statement that Christ was a man. The *masculine* form of the word we are apt to think about, yet it is evident that the masculine does not exhaust the full conception of humanity—the feminine must be there as well. Can we not say, then, that in a complete sense Christ was *human?* The womanly mind and the manly mind may centre in him alike, for he has in himself the peculiarities of both mental natures. The humanity of Christ is so perfect that the vigor of the man and the grace of the woman are blended together in a most finished manner. But this is not all. Christ has in himself all the good of *all varieties* of men and women. He represents the entire race, and fits the entire race. Christ may be called the universal man. He heads up in himself the greatest number of characteristics. It has been said of Shakspeare that his greatness consisted in this, that "many men may commune with him who cannot commune with one another." In a far higher and holier sense is this true of Christ. He was many sided. All excellencies centered in him. The most diverse traits found in him a unity. Christ needed more than one writer to portray him. And even the four who have sketched his life would have failed if inspiration had not assisted. In fact, the life of Christ has not yet been written. No man shall ever be able to write it. There is a *something* about the Redeemer that cannot be seized, that cannot be described. We cannot balance him as he is balanced; the order and equilibrium of his being we cannot set forth. As even God is more glorious than his own universe makes him appear to be, so Christ is far above any of the human pictures that are designed to represent him.

But if Christ is human, he is also *divine*. The sympathy of Christ has no special adaptation to the wants of man unless that sympathy be divine as well as human. A mere man, however good or however great, in Palestine or paradise, is really not what the soul wants. Strictly speaking, it is neither the sympathy of man by himself nor of God by himself that meets the cry of a wounded humanity, but it is the sympathy of the God-man. Whenever I look to the human side of Jesus and take encouragement from that, the encouragement really springs up out of the divine in connection with the human. The sympathy of Christ is *theanthropical*.

But our views of the world's Consoler will be heightened if we notice a certain *symbolism* that points out his *deep humiliation* and his *exalted nature*. As this idea of symbolism in connection with the life of Christ is somewhat suggestive, it will repay us to glance at it in its twofold aspect.

First, then, let us note down those symbolic circumstances that point to the *humiliation* of the Son of God. At the very commencement, we think of the lowly circumstances that connected themselves with the advent of Christ. His mother was neither rich nor learned. The holy child is born in a stable, is cradled in a manger. We are startled that one so great should appear in the midst of surroundings that matched not with the greatness. Who would suppose that darkness and debasement would mark and line the place where the Anointed One should first open his eyes among men? If we had been called upon to draw out the first scenes in the life of Jesus, with only our reason to guide us, the veritable realities of the case would never have trooped past our vision. Yea, we should have thought that such a lofty visitor would have made his home among the great, with everything to make pleasant the hours of helpless infancy. The first feeling, then, is that of surprise. The outward scenery *does not seem to correspond with the greatness* and royalty of the divine child. And yet, the moment the full meaning of the incarnation dawns upon the mind, there is seen to be a wonderful adaptation in the earthly surroundings of Jesus. The Son of God had descended to the very bottom of the race, and everything must be called in to bear witness to this fact.

Mark now the hasty departure into Egypt. The holy family flee away by night. What a picture; and how that picture is shaded! Years pass away. The divine man is working at the trade of a carpenter. To say the least, this is wonderful. If such a scene images forth humiliation, it no less images forth greatness. Labor is dignified forever. Behold Christ now in the wilderness. He is surrounded by wild beasts and malignant angels. All outward good is taken away. The gloom of forty days, the deeper gloom of forty nights, darken his solitude. Again, during the public life of Christ, we are told that "he had not where to lay his head." The Possessor of all things has nothing! Still further, a painful moment in the life of Jesus is revealed,—a moment that seems like the anticipation of Gethsemane. "Now is my soul troubled; and what shall I say? Father, save me from this hour: but for this cause came I unto this hour." A door is opened into the mysterious chamber of Christly emotion. We are told to look in. We do so with awe and amazement; and at once the door is shut. There is Christ in the garden. "He sweats as it were great drops of blood falling down to the ground." The whole scene is more fit for silent meditation than for direct portrayal. Then, again, Christ is on trial. The Creator stands before the creature, the Sinless before the sinful. The Holy One is pronounced guilty. The Judge of all is condemned. The Life must die. There is the crown of thorns and the cross; the darkness at noon and the fearful cry, "My God, my God, why hast thou forsaken me?" The symbolism of death and darkness ends with the shaking of the earth and the rending asunder of the rocks.

Secondly, we may now consider that symbolism which points to the *divine* in Christ. There were flashes of supernatural light that shot athwart the sky of the Son of God and Son of man. The day broke in upon the night. Heaven touched the earth. It could be seen that the tabernacle of God was with man. Even at the birth of Christ a star appeared, betokening the advent of some great personage.

Then there was a *glory of the Lord* that shone round the astonished shepherds at night, an angel that announced good tidings of joy, a multitude of heavenly beings "praising God, and saying, Glory to God in the highest, and on earth peace, good will toward men." We can perceive also hints of the divine when Christ was in the temple in the midst of the doctors. The temple was the culmination and crown of Judaism; and it stood forth as the mystic symbol of a divine redemption. It was not strange, therefore, that the youthful Jesus should linger in such a place; and that, possessed with the one thought of his life, he should say to his astonished parents, "Wist ye not that I must be about my Father's business?" Then at his baptism we are arrested by a supernatural scene. The heavens open, the Spirit of God descends, and a voice says, "This is my beloved Son in whom I am well pleased." Saying nothing here of the miracles of Christ, we meet with such expressions as these: "The people were astonished at his doctrine." "The multitudes marvelled, and glorified God." "Never man spake like this man." "Is not this the Christ?" "Truly this man was the Son of God." Was there not also a sense of something superhuman when he drove the money-changers out of the temple? as if the men were awed by a great presence, so that they hastened away. But perhaps the most striking symbolism is that connected with the transfiguration scene. The face of the Redeemer "shone as the sun, and his raiment was white as the light." Two saved men appeared from the heavenly world. The voice of God pealed forth from the excellent glory, saying, "This is my beloved Son, in whom I am well pleased." Everything here was so wonderful that the disciples "fell on their face, and were sore afraid." Again, we have an incident mentioned by one of the gospel writers that may have a relation to the point before us. Judas, with a band of armed men had come to arrest the Saviour. They no sooner, however, appear in his presence, and he makes known to them that he is the person they are in search of, than they step backward, and fall to the ground. A thought of something great, whatever it was, seems to have intimidated them for a moment; so that they lost their balance, staggered, and fell. Even the dream of Pilate's wife has about it a dim inkling of the supernatural. The words, "Have thou nothing to do with that just man," sound like the spent-utterance of a divine voice that had pressed through from eternity into time. The title on the cross is itself suggestive.—"THIS IS JESUS THE KING OF THE JEWS." It is not strange that the chief priests were dissatisfied with it. As a closing picture, we have the following: The graves were opened; many bodies of the saints arose; they entered into the holy city. An event so mighty as a finished atonement thrilled the heavenly kingdoms of life and startled the empire of death, so that eager beings hurried through the gates of glory and the grave, and stood forth among living men as witnesses of a Redeemer's power and a resurrection yet to be.

Such is the twofold symbolism that wraps itself like clouds of glory and of gloom about the Saviour's life. A Being thus circumstanced is preëminently the great Sympathizer. To see the Saviour in this double manner throws new meaning upon his life, and brings him nearer to the soul.

A thought now in regard to the *temptation* of Christ, as that relates to the theme in hand. There are those who cannot see how Christ could be tempted, inasmuch as he was perfectly holy. No doubt a depraved nature is that which gives nerve and point to much of the temptation of life; but it by no means explains the whole matter. That Christ was a *man* was sufficient to constitute a ground of temptation. Though he was a sinless man, he yet had *natural appetites:* temptation could appeal to them. He had the *love of honor*, of course in its purity: temptation could appeal to that. There was in his soul a *love of power*, equally in its purity: temptation could appeal to that also. Then he had a nature that was capable of *suffering:* temptation could certainly work there with great power. Now, if the wilderness-temptation of Christ be examined, it will be seen that there was an attempt to twist appetite, honor, and power from their normal position; while the nature that shrunk from suffering was assailed all the way through life; chiefly, however, during that great crisis when the Redeemer cried out, "If it be possible, let this cup pass from me: nevertheless, not as I will, but as thou wilt." Let the temptations of man now be systematized, and it will be discovered that they can be reduced to a few generic heads. How much of sin by yielding to the appetites. A world of iniquity has been committed here sufficient to sink the world. As to honor, that has taken captive the whole race. The love of power has filled the earth with contention. Then to avoid suffering, how wickedness has been followed and principle sacrificed. This being the case, the tempted Saviour fits the tempted sinner. "We have not a high priest which cannot be touched with the feeling of our infirmities; but was in all points tempted like as we are, yet without sin."

We may now glance at the *solitude* of Jesus. A certain writer has remarked that there is always a degree of solitude about great minds. There is truth in this thought. They live in a sphere of being by themselves, and their course of thinking no one fully comprehends; their manner of life, transcending that of common men, being out of the plane of the world's doings and duties, is not known. Such persons tarry with us, yet we understand them not; we see them, yet we see them not. Like lofty strangers they come and disappear; like visitors from some higher world they pass through among us, and then vanish away; the full vision of their being and greatness never falling upon any soul of man; so that few rejoice when they come, and fewer sorrow when they depart. Their personality is to us like a dream of night, which, when the day appears, is but dimly remembered. Especially was solitude of existence a characteristic of Jesus. "His soul was like a star and dwelt apart." He had a mission and a plan which not one of the human family could understand. There was not a single individual to whom he could reveal the contents of his wonderful mind with the hope of finding an intelligent approval. Although he lived upon the earth, he seemed not to be one of its people. He was as a solitary stranger from some remote and unknown territory of Jehovah's empire. The nature of his being and the nature of his work were alike unique, and so he acted in solitude, the lofty representative of some superior world. It made no difference that thousands followed in his train; for whether he dwelt in "the void waste or the city full" he was yet alone. Yea, the oppressive loneliness of his being was only increased by the presence of men; men who were dull, unsympathizing, and frequently sceptical touching the embassy which brought him from heaven to earth. The divine man commenced and finished the mightiest work of the universe alone. He was aided by no human arm. Not even a single, whole-hearted encouragement cheered him along his path. He suffered and died for a world of sinners in profound solitude. A being thus situated, and thus acting, has a soul to pity where no pity is wanted, and a compassion to exercise towards the most abandoned of men that awakens no thankfulness or praise. Sympathy reaches a height of grandeur, when forgotten and unappreciated it toils and travails for the eternal good of a world.

Again, Christ was "*a man of sorrows.*" To those natures who have in them an element of sadness, there is something in the idea of a sorrowful Saviour that is attractive. I scarcely know anything that throws such a soft sacredness about the person of our Lord as the fact that sorrow found an abiding home in his spirit. That the Sinless One should be sorrowful is really surprising. The mind is startled by it. Afterwards it is stilled. A kind of sad composure comes over the soul while thinking of the fact of sorrow in the Son of God. Ideally we might think of Christ in a thousand ways and connect with his being a thousand glories, yet the beauty of sorrow with its pain we should imagine to be no trait of his. Certainly, the more he is studied, he appears as the redemptive man; having a life that was sacrificial; being the sorrowful Sufferer of humanity. He lived and wept, not for himself, but for man. Though holy, his sorrow was deeper and more pungent than that which agitated the breast of any sinner. He was "baptized in the cloud and in the sea." His pilgrimage was but one *Via Dolorosa.* To say that Christ had a sympathetic nature will not explain the totality of his grief. There was a sorrow that lay deeper than that caused by natural sympathy. Christ was supernatural, and his sorrow was redemptive. Although the divine nature of the Redeemer could not sorrow, yet the human nature was able to sustain a mightier load of grief by reason of its connection with the divine. Rightly understood, the sorrow of Christ was *superhuman,* though *not divine.* It was superhuman in the sense that no mere human being could have endured it. Salvation has its life in sorrow, and Christianity is the religion of sorrow.

As a closing thought, we may fix the eye on the *serenity* of Christ. Some might suppose that sorrow and serenity do not go together, inasmuch as gloom is apt to be connected with sorrow. Gloom may to a certain extent connect itself with it among men, but with Christ there was nothing of the kind. Even among the purer and better natures of earth who have sorrow, there is nothing dark and forbidding. It is really a question whether any human countenance is perfect in its expression without a certain tinge of sadness. There is a place, then, for both sorrow and serenity in Christ. In his nature there was no element of discontent. There was no shadow at variance between the human and the divine will. The principle of unity was complete. Christ's spiritual consciousness was perfectly clear. Serenitude, therefore, had no cloud. With a weight of obligation such as the world cannot conceive and a sense of obligation such as the world cannot feel, he was yet unruffled in his mind. That the burden he carried was great and the suffering he endured was keen, is evident at a glance. He was pressed to the dust by reason of the weight of a world's atonement. The surging billows of divine wrath beat against him as the one who stood in the room of the guilty. Still, there was no impatience manifested. Intense pain, though it caused his human nature to cry out, scattered not away the heavenly serenity of his soul. Calm and divine-like he came out of the storm. There was a sweetness of mind and manner, a heavenly radiance, a divine repose. Though he was the great warrior of men, the marks of battle were not found upon his spirit. The sympathy of such a Redeemer is complete.

PART II.

Voices of the Soul answered in God the Restorer.

CHAPTER I.

VESTIGES OF THE DIVINE IN MAN NOT SUFFICIENT TO DEVELOP HOLINESS APART FROM THE SUPERNATURAL.

THERE is much said and written about the godlike elements that still exist in human nature. We no sooner begin to speak of the depth and universality of sin than we are arrested by the statement, "that man is good as well as bad." The least whisper touching the need of the supernatural is hushed at once by the certain announcement, that such language is mere superstition; dishonorable both to God and man as it tends to develop a vain dependence, instead of that hopefulness of souls which is inspired by the divine that is in them. With much fine writing on the dignity and ultimate blessedness of all mankind, we have not yet seen the record of those varied rudiments of life and love which are to grow and spread till sin is dead. The most serious writer of this school is Dr. Channing; the most daring is Theodore Parker. The *true* divine undertones of the soul which these men point out, we admit; their inferences from them, we, in most cases, deny. It is proposed in the present chapter to gather together the most important fragments of the divine which the soul contains, that we may thus see whether they are sufficient or not to form the independent basis of a perfect character.

1. We may notice the craving of the soul for rest. It is doubtful whether any man ever sinks so low in moral degradation as to be wholly unconscious of the yearning of his spirit for repose. We think there is a cry ascending from every heart for peace that knows no turmoil, and for rest that knows no strife or tumult of men. This feeling arises in the soul because unhappiness is there; and it would seem to show that there is a higher and better nature which is crushed and in bondage; for why should there be a longing and panting after an unknown joy, unless it be that the immortal spirit is discontented with its present state and circumstances? It is the divine in man that longs for a good which it has not, and is

dissatisfied with an evil which it has. That strange feeling of restlessness which agitates the bosom of mortals, which makes many a heart to bleed unseen and causes many a sigh to ascend unheard, is doubtless the fluttering of a greater spirit than that which spends its hours in the enjoyment of sense, and its days in the eager pursuit of pleasure and sin.

2. There is in the soul also a desire for unmixed truth. It is necessary for man to have an appetency of this kind, in order to connect the soul with the vast region of truth which is all around it. Pure knowledge is increased by this means, for pure truth is the object of search and solicitude. Neither science nor scientific investigation could exist if men had not the desire for simple truth. One could not put confidence in another without a primary conviction in the mind that truth would be uttered. A child, at first, will believe every statement of a father or mother. Even if a stranger comes into the house, and in a thoughtless manner promises a gift to each child the next time he comes, all will believe his words, and will be greatly disappointed if, when he appears again, the promised favor is not forthcoming.

3. There is a law of order existing in all minds. The soul cannot be satisfied with disharmony. Even noise troubles some persons exceedingly; but music is pleasing. An ill-regulated family is a source of uneasiness to a spectator. Even a child will instinctively arrange its playthings on the floor in a certain line, and will place those together that are alike. This law of order is seen in its divine aspect when the soul is made to feel happy in view of its good, and miserable in view of its evil. An archetype of order exists in the mind so complete in itself that nothing created comes fully up to its demands; it finds no realization save in the Uncreated and the Perfect.

4. Greatness calls forth the admiration of even the lowest of men. Physical might and power, at first, attract the attention; afterwards, greatness and sweep of intellect. Brilliant pictures of the imagination and grand thoughts of the understanding generate enthusiasm and wonder in the minds both of the ignorant and the wise. Admiration is also awakened by the sight of noble and heroic deeds. Let one but endure the utmost self-denial and suffer the most excruciating pain in order to benefit the needy, and instantly the vilest are compelled

to praise such self-abnegation. Hence a monument must be erected to commemorate the deeds of Howard; eulogies on the life of Socrates must be written and sung. Yea, more, where can you find a sceptic who does not admire the perfect character of Jesus? Prejudice and passion may distort the mind, but they cannot destroy the divine nature within.

5. The soul has a conception of the beautiful. This is a ray shining out from the better sphere of being. While beauty is seen in nature and art, yet it is chiefly spiritual beauty that we are here concerned with. This higher conception is like one of the lamps of heaven, burning amidst the darkness of perdition. Says Mr. Parker: "To the mind God will be the Beauty of Truth; to the conscience the Beauty of Justice, to the affection the Beauty of Love, to the soul the Beauty of Holiness, and to the whole consciousness of man he will appear as the total Infinite Beauty; the perfect and absolute object of every hungering faculty of man." *

6. The human spirit has aspirations which run out to the eternal and the infinite. It is true that like children men oftentimes play

* "Theism, Atheism, and the Popular Theology," p. 187.

along the shore, heedless of that vast ocean on whose bosom they must sail forever. Yet it is certain that there are desires which the present cannot satisfy; and the good that is not found to-day is supposed to have an abiding dwelling-place in some to-morrow. The ever-hungering and ever-traveling aspirations of man show that he was made for a lofty sphere; for although the earth may flow with plenty and time may extend its benefactions to the last moment, yet is there even then a want felt, plainly revealing the fact that the supersensible and the infinite alone can satisfy. "I affirm, and trust that I do not speak too strongly, that there are traces of infinity in the human mind; and that, in this very respect, it bears a likeness to God. The very conception of infinity is the mark of a nature to which no limit can be prescribed. This thought, indeed, comes to us, not so much from abroad, as from our own souls. We ascribe this attribute to God, because we possess capacities and wants, which only an unbounded being can fill, and because we are conscious of a tendency in spiritual faculties to unlimited expansion."*

7. Man also has the idea of religion. The

* Dr. Channing, Works, vol. iii, p. 237.

fact that religion of some kind is found among all nations and races, shows that the idea is natural. We must think that man was made to be religious. He has an idea of a supernatural Being, and it is his own fault if he does not reverence and worship that Being. A whole world with no belief in God and no form of religion would be one of the most astonishing sights in the universe. Worship of some kind will never cease to be offered.

8. Each soul has the intuitions of right and justice. Actions are viewed as good or bad, as praiseworthy or blameworthy. In all the relations of life man must be just; and the righteous must be rewarded, the wicked punished. But notice chiefly a very interesting manifestation of these principles. Let one, for instance, see nothing but selfishness and dishonesty around him, will he be wholly pleased and contented with these characteristics? He will not. He will in his heart wish to be among a better class of people. "Men do weary of the wickedness of the world as really, though not indeed so frequently, as of its disappointments. This is not the place for labored discussion; and I will simply refer you to one powerful instance of this anxiety for a

better and holier condition. I allude to cases of *private and personal injury.* Reflect upon your emotions in such instances. There is surely something more than mere resentment; there is a strong sense of injustice, and naturally with it (as the mind calms and diffuses its feelings) a melancholy impression of the lost moral balance of the whole world, and a correspondent yearning for abodes where righteousness shall be a principle of universal action." *

9. It is worthy of careful consideration also that the soul calls for the manifestation of personal benevolence. No man can be satisfied with himself unless some efforts are made in the line of duty and love. Hence, in one way and another, men are trying their hand at good works. It is really astonishing to see how universal is this habit among mankind. To do evil is certainly not deemed the chief end of man. The most wicked profess to be good, at times. Even the thief feels that he is benevolent, if he gives a part of his plunder to the poor; and the avaricious man claims the same characteristic, if once in a while he assists the needy. There is no end to good men. Absolute selfishness so terrifies the race that each

* Prof. Butler, Sermons, vol. ii. p. 152.

one has his coat of charity. It would be a relief to see a bad man. In the intense eagerness of persons to be righteous, they have made the evil good.

10. In all men there are attempts at self-reformation. This is a most striking fact. It shows that personal depravity does not satisfy the better nature of the soul. Doubtless, in some cases, man tries to live a purer life, merely to gain the approval of those around him. But this is not the constant motive. There is in the breast a sense of spirit-worthiness which excites to self-purification. However fair one may appear to others, this is not enough; for there may be with it a secret abhorrence of self, as if a divinity were dwelling within the soul and watching all its motives and moral states, casting a frown upon the invisible evil that may be found there. All know that there are moments when man does despise himself; and surely it is not strange that, at such times, he should hasten to begin the work of moral improvement. Besides, he may have a vision of God and eternity so clear and strong that his whole nature is aroused; and he looks around with eager eyes that he may watch against the evil, and that he may attend to the good.

11. The feeling of remorse evinces the existence of a divine element in the soul. I cannot see why the spirit should condemn and torment itself for wrong-doing, if there be not a voice within which utters its command against evil, and which speaks in favor of the good. Remorse would be impossible, if the soul did not affirm the necessity of goodness. Hence, let a man sink ever so deep in moral degradation, and yet be conscious of guilt, this is proof that the divine principle still lives. "The evil conscience is the divine bond which binds the created spirit, even in deep apostacy, to its Original. In the consciousness of guilt there is revealed the essential relation of our spirit to God. The trouble and anguish which the remonstrances of this consciousness excite, the inward unrest which sometimes seizes the slave of sin, are proofs that he has not got quite broken away from God." *

12. We even see phantoms of goodness associated with certain sins. It might appear as if we were pressing the matter to an extreme when we thus attempt to find gold in the midst of mire. Our intention in this last effort is to give man all that belongs to him. Ob-

* Müller, "Doctrine of Sin," vol. i. p. 225.

serve, then, the vast variety of acts wrong in themselves, yet performed with the utmost sincerity. Murder is even committed with the approval of conscience. The idea of right is here, although there is nothing but wrong. Idolatry itself suggests a good which it has not, even as a tombstone reflects the light that comes from afar. Worshipping a multitude of gods, instead of the one Divinity, shows that however much the religious instinct may be darkened, it yet cannot be destroyed. As the deluded creature bows before his idol, the fact is announced that here is a being who ought to worship the Supreme. In selfishness men are anxious not to appear selfish. This plainly shows that disinterestedness is thought to be a good thing. How the wicked also desire to have a good name. This striking fact can have no meaning, unless it is admitted that virtue is deemed superior to vice. Thus, in the midst of the ruins of the soul, we behold apparitions of good.

It is not needful that I specify further. The most important thoughts have been mentioned; and whatever has been omitted may find a place under some of the previous heads. Are these divine characteristics, then, sufficient to develop a holy life? What arrests the attention is the fact, that men of the most finished depravity have these vestiges of the divine. Why so much of wickedness, if good seed is planted in the soul? Can men sink to the lowest depths of sin, while there is a moral efficiency in the heart that can save them? It is clear that there must be a power in human nature that exceeds in might the native potency of that which is divine. I can see nothing in the symptoms of a better nature within but so many proofs of moral weakness. It is not difficult to conceive that souls may increase in sin through myriads of ages, and yet have visions of a better state floating before them, and cries for the true and the good sounding forth from a nature that no more can die than the mind of which it forms a part. I may as well reason out the future possibility of holiness from the existence of a soul, as from the natural principles that constitute but a portion of it. On examination it will be seen that each relic of the divine has an intuitional or instinctive basis; and consequently, we can no more infer from such the prospective attainment of moral perfection, than we can from the mere existence of a human will or a human conscience. The mind has natural powers and principles without which moral action is not even possible; but this is an entirely different thing from right moral action itself. That I shall ever use these powers and principles to work out an eternal righteousness is what no one can know. My disposition and choice may make it certain that I will not use them for holiness and God.

Yea, I am startled by a very clear law of *moral deterioration* existent in the race; so that, instead of ascending, they evermore have a tendency to descend. Admitting a development in science, art, civilization, and many other things, our wonder is that in holiness the race do not improve. True, among the Christian nations, there is spiritual advancement; but that we attribute to the inflow of the supernatural. Among men in general there is *spiritual indifference;* and *communion with God* is not known. Development-men exalt the present and depress the past; yet no credit is given to Christianity as a divine system. "The real starting point," remarks Comte, "is in fact much humbler than is commonly supposed, man having everywhere begun by being a fetich worshipper and a cannibal." *

* Positive Phil. p. 545.

I should like to know how this information has been received. History does not convey it to us. The statement is baseless. Proof is demanded. If I pretend to give an account of the planting and training of the race, I must be regulated by fact, and not by fancy. The earliest authentic record that we have, shows that man began his existence pure and holy; that he had knowledge of but one God, the Creator and Sovereign; that the golden age was at the beginning, which he lost by sin; that then the Divine Being was worshipped by sacrifices, each man being a priest; that afterwards the race deteriorated to such an extent that they were swept away by the retributive justice of the Almighty. This whole view harmonizes with geologic history. Hugh Miller says: "We know,—so far at least as we have yet succeeded in deciphering the record,—that the several dynasties were introduced, not in their lower, but in their higher forms; that, in short, in the imposing programme of creation it was arranged, as a general rule, that in each of the great divisions of the procession the magnates should walk first." And as if to shadow forth most truly the condition of man, "we recognize yet further the fact of degradation specially exemplified in the fish and the reptile." *

But decay and moral ruin are seen in the most striking manner as we look at the refined nations of antiquity. We should naturally think that with the highest civilization, there would be the highest type of moral life. And this the more as men are understood to be born with original righteousness. It is manifestly a dark sign when neither subjective goodness on the one hand, nor objective advantages on the other, can lift man up to a state of perfect rectitude; but with both he must plunge into the deepest moral degradation. Notice what the historian says touching the manners of Greece and Rome: "The lives of men of every class, from the highest to the lowest, were consumed in the practice of the most abominable and flagitious vices: even crimes, the horrible turpitude of which was such that it would be defiling the ear of decency but to name them, were openly perpetrated with the greatest impunity. If evidence be required of this, the reader may at once satisfy himself of the truth of what is here said by referring to Lucian amongst the Greek authors,

* "Foot-prints of the Creator," p. 325.

and to the Roman poets Juvenal and Persius. In the writings of the former in particular, he will find the most detestable unnatural affections, treated of at large, and with the utmost familiarity, as things of ordinary and daily occurrence. Should any one conceive that these or other writers might give the rein too freely to their imagination, and suffer themselves to be carried into extremes by their genius for satire and sharp rebuke, let him turn his attention to those cruel and inhuman exhibitions which are well known to have yielded the highest gratification to the inhabitants of Greece and Italy, (people, who in point of refinement, possessed a superiority over all other nations of the world,) the savage conflicts of the gladiators in the circus: let him cast his eye on that dissoluteness of manners by which the walks of private life were polluted; the horrible prostitution of boys, to which the laws opposed no restraint, the shameful practice of exposing infants and procuring abortions; the little regard that was shown to the lives of slaves; the multiplicity of stews and brothels, many of which were consecrated even to the gods themselves. Let him reflect on these, and various other criminal excesses, to the most ample indulgence in which the government offered not the least impediment, and then say, if such were the people distinguished beyond all others by the excellence of their laws and the superiority of their attainments in literature and the arts, what must have been the state of those nations who possessed none of these advantages, but were governed entirely by the impulses and dictates of rude and uncultivated nature." * When one thus sees the most noted of ancient nations sinking by the collective weight of their iniquity till finally they disappear from the page of history, it is all in vain to speak of the restorative energy of latent goodness. A theory of human nature that runs counter, not to a few facts, but to many, cannot be true.

And what are we to think of the existence of *savages*, with the same theory before us? If the good in man is so powerful, why have whole races sunk even lower than the brute? Why all this, too, although a period of *six thousand years* has been allowed for human development? This is strange progress! The development is in ignorance and sin; it is downward, and not upward. A very curious

* Mosheim, "Historical Commentaries," vol. i. p. 26.

fact is noted by Professor Guyot and others that the further we depart from the cradle of the race in Asia, the race deteriorates physically. Hence the inhabitants at the extreme point of South America are vastly lower than those further north. So the Bushmen of Southern Africa are even inferior to the Hottentots. And when we reach the dwellers of South Australia, we behold the lowest of the human species. Body and mind go down together. We cannot see much force, then, in speaking of divine barbarians, of saintly cannibals. And what is worse, these brutalized people can never lift themselves out of their condition. History has never witnessed the phenomenon of a community of savages changing themselves into civilized, enlightened, upright men. "The human mind," in the language of Isaac Taylor, "contains no law of development taking effect as a constant physical law. Development of the faculties, intellectual and social, is, in every individual man, and in nations and races, contingent upon the presence and application of some exciting cause from without." "The expansion of the human mind does not take place uniformly and universally for this very reason: that a causative power having been conferred upon man—and upon him alone, in the fullest sense, among the animal orders—no other provision has been made in his constitution for securing the development of his faculties. This inherent force is amply sufficient for this purpose, if only it be put in movement *from without*." "The fate of the individual man truly symbolizes the history or the fate of nations and races. A tribe—a race, marked as the same from age to age by its physical characteristics, occupies or roams about upon its unfurrowed allotment until the day of awakening from without dawns upon it; or, if no such day dawns, the race becomes extinct, or it gives room to another that has received the quickening visitation from a higher source." *

The supernatural, then, would seem to be absolutely necessary. Fully admitting that man has relics of the divine within him, yet these are powerless. To look up is now the part of wisdom. From above, a power and a life must come down. Indeed, to be truthful, we ought to mention the demand for the supernatural as one of the divine vestiges of the soul. This demand often shows itself in a very

* "World of Mind," p. 371.

peculiar manner,—in a sigh of the soul while thinking of the vanity of life, in a feeling of dissatisfaction with mere legalism however exact it may be, in a sense of want that often arises after man has done his best, and in a sinking heart-sickness produced by the blasting of human hopes and the utter wickedness of human souls. Men sometimes do not know what is wrong with the religious system which they adopt or with the religious life which they practice; only this is certain—they feel uneasy —they want something they know not what. The truth is, mere naturalism cannot satisfy. The race have ever wanted a divine religion. Even wicked men find a degree of satisfaction in supernatural verities. Though practically they may care nothing about them, yet their higher nature is pleased. The Bible will ever be new and ever fresh, because the eternal and the divine run through it. The Christian religion will never vanish away, because its supernatural redemption and profound mysteries appeal to the very soul of the race. The sabbath with its preaching about God, man, and the Mediator, will be perpetuated till it loses itself in the eternal rest of heaven. A mere day without work, with its philosophical lectures, will never fully satisfy the sin-crushed soul. Even simple ethical preaching will become insipid. The cry will be for a Power that can meet human weakness, and a Saviour that can cancel human sin. The thought of a great Presence touching souls; the solemnity that spreads over the mind when the Almighty is passing by; the stillness that reigns around when it is felt that the eternal God is at work in human hearts,—these peculiarities awe and satisfy the spirit of man.

CHAPTER II.

NATURAL BENEVOLENCE NOT SUFFICIENT TO CONSTITUTE HOLINESS APART FROM THE SUPERNATURAL.

Objection has arisen to the doctrine of total depravity because it seems to set aside certain benevolent features of human nature. We propose, therefore, to mention those traits of the human being which are really lovely in themselves, that we may thus behold the truth, and know what value to attach to it. We would give each man all that belongs to him. If there be sunshine as well as shade, let us rejoice.

1. We may notice the *family affections.* There is something very beautiful in beholding a mother watching over a little infant during the years of its helplessness. To see the care taken, the self-denial endured, and that without murmuring, is certainly a pleasant sight.

The love is warm, strong, and abiding. The very suffering incidentally connected with the relation of mother and child seems to fan the affection into a more burning intensity. Through long, weary nights she watches beside the little one in its sickness. Perhaps the health of the parent is giving way through excessive vigils; yet this does not abate the love in the least,—it is stronger than death. On the part of the children, the love is not so ardent nor so strong; yet, as far as it goes, it is sweet to look upon. The lamp of affection goes not out. If there is to be a difference in degree between the parental and the filial love, it seems the part of wisdom that the parental should be the stronger. There is more need for it on the one side than on the other. Children have not to toil and to suffer for parents, as parents for children.

2. *Sympathy for others in distress* is another beautiful feature of humanity. A man has just fallen from a building: how eagerly all hasten to assist him! A railroad collision has just taken place; many are wounded and killed: how deep the sympathy of the spectators! A child has fallen into the river from a steamboat; instantly it is saved by one at

the risk of his life: how profound the interest of all on board! Here is a family perishing; they have neither food, fuel, nor clothing: those beholding them weep. In sickness and death, how tender and sacred is the sympathy manifested! To see a group of mourners around a grave weeping, is a hallowed sight in a world of sin and death. A man without sympathy is deemed a monster: a woman without pity is considered a demon.

3. *Amiability of disposition* is a lovely characteristic of human nature. There are only a few persons who are gifted with this beautiful trait. It is not so general as sympathy. Here and there we see one smiling upon us like a flower in the forest. The soft gentle words, and the kind modest look speak eloquently to the heart. There is nothing harsh or repelling in the manner,—all is inviting. In little children this trait is seen. Men seldom possess it. Women have it the most. It seems more in harmony with the female character than the male. Yet no man is complete without it.

4. *A nice sense of honor* is commendable also wherever found. There is much fictitious honor among men. Still, we must admit that

there is true honor. Some persons possess a certain native nobleness which makes a fine impression on the mind. Such individuals practice none of those little, mean acts which so disfigure the characters of many. They dispute not about trifles; they count not a man an enemy for a word; they trample not on the rights of others. There seems to be in their minds a sense of fitness, which instinctively teaches them how to act. Wherever one finds true honor, he finds also manliness.

5. *The love of country* very properly comes in here. That there is such a feeling, all admit. It is natural for one to love the land of his birth. The feeling grows up imperceptibly with the growth of the mind. Love of country would seem to be an extension of the love of home. Man is first a son, then a citizen. The parental government is preparatory and auxiliary to the civil government. Patriotism is always held in honor when manifested in its purity. It is right that it should be, as it is difficult to find one who is truly patriotic. The feeling is very apt to mingle with others less pure, as a clear rill loses itself in the turbid river.

6. *Friendship* is worthy of all praise. There is a law of affinity running through the universe.

Like tends to like. In matter and mind this holds true. One may have many acquaintances, but few friends. The soul loves concentration. The heart loves unity. One may say, Good-morning or Good-evening to many; yet the salutation which tells of the soul's day and night is spoken in the ears of a select few. Perhaps the communions of the spirit are best rehearsed in the hearing of but one kindred mind. There is more of sacred secrecy when one only is at your side; it is an intrusion for others to draw near. David was contented with Jonathan; Damon with Pythias. Aristotle says: "Those friendships which are most celebrated, are between two only. Those who have many friends, and are familiar with everybody, are by no one thought to be friends, except in a political sense; and these are called men-pleasers." * It is not certain, however, that one friend is all that man craves.

7. *The philanthropic spirit* next demands attention. This is the love of man as man. One who has this spirit seeks to remove the evils which press upon humanity. There are but few distinguished philanthropists. The fact that the word suggests, only a name, here

* Nicom. Ethics, b. ix. c. x. Transl. by Prof. Browne.

and there, shows this. In private life there are persons whose bosoms burn with a truly philanthropic love; but they are never heard of beyond their own little circle of acquaintances. The feeling sometimes loses itself in that of hospitality, as being the only way it can manifest itself under the circumstances.

8. We may close our list by noticing the feeling of *gratitude.* It is a law of gratitude that it can only exist in view of a disinterested act. The moment we realize that one is selfish in his gift, we cannot feel grateful. We rather abhor the man who is seeking praise through the guise of beneficence. Lord Kames notices a very peculiar characteristic pertaining to gratitude. He says: "A signal act of gratitude produces in the spectator or reader, not only love or esteem for the author, but also a separate feeling, being a vague feeling of gratitude, without an object—a feeling however that disposes the spectator or reader to acts of gratitude, more than upon an ordinary occasion." "The feeling is singular in the following respect—that it is accompanied with a desire to perform acts of gratitude, without having any object; though in that state, the mind, wonderfully bent on an object, neglects no oppor-

tunity to vent itself: any act of kindness or good will, that would pass unregarded upon another occasion, is greedily seized; and the vague feeling is converted into a real passion of gratitude: in such a state, favors are returned double."*

These features of natural goodness are the most important; and we need not enlarge. The point for us now to settle is the *moral quality* of all this benevolence.

No one will deny that it is purely natural for a mother to love her children, and purely natural also for one to feel sympathy for another in distress. These feelings are very strong, even much stronger than the affections of our moral nature; yet for all this they spring forth spontaneously. The wisdom of God is seen in this marked arrangement of human nature. He has done for the family and for those in distress what we never would have done, if we simply were possessed of a moral nature. As to the propriety of calling these natural affections *benevolent*, there may be a question. We certainly do not speak of a benevolent bear or tiger, although these animals have natural affections. Dogs have performed deeds which al-

* "Elements of Criticism," chap. ii. part i.

most shame out of existence the actions of man, yet we are not willing to speak of benevolent dogs. From the nature of the case, then, the word benevolence is used in an inferior sense when it is applied to the working of the instinctive feelings. The *sound* of the word, we suppose, has deluded many; for they have thought themselves morally good, when in fact they were only naturally good.

Moreover, it must be admitted that an act cannot be virtuous unless it springs from a *virtuous principle.* When we see the *most wicked men,* then, manifesting natural benevolence, we are compelled to conclude that it has no virtuous foundation. Such men can have love and pity, and yet be the most perfect villains. They care nothing about virtue; they oppose it; they at heart dislike it; while they have a peculiar relish for the most sinful indulgences. Now, this would be impossible if true goodness existed in the soul. If a man loves his friend, and is grateful to his benefactor, because a holy principle prompts him to act in this way, how is it that he has a fixed aversion to the pure and the good at the same time? Surely if one has true love, he will love the lovely wherever it is found, and hate that which is opposed to it. If a divine principle of benevolence were the root and spring of all the special affections, then, we should expect to see each man loving God supremely, and his neighbor as himself; but it is very certain that millions care neither for God nor man. We cannot, then, make human beings truly benevolent at so cheap a rate. It is the grand peculiarity of a holy principle in the heart that it makes the subject of it love *all* creatures. In the nature of things it can have no limit. The moment you limit a holy principle, that moment you take away its peculiar quality. If I am a good man, I must love all beings according to their standing in the universe, and must love holiness wherever I find it. It would be absurd for me to say, "I love the men who are around me, and hate all others; I love the holiness which is manifested in my neighborhood, and hate that which exists beyond it." The conclusion then is, that if one does not love outside of the sphere of the special affections, he does not possess divine love at all. A holy affection is not confined to the finite; it rests only when it has reached the Infinite.

Perhaps we may be asked just here, if sympathy for the distressed and love for a child are never truly good feelings? We answer, that all the instinctive feelings may be truly good when a virtuous principle enters into and directs them. If one can love his children so as to train them up for God and eternity, then, most assuredly this is good. If one's gratitude is the outgoing of a benevolent heart, it is praiseworthy. All the affections can be sanctified. There may be a sanctified philanthropy like that of John Howard's, and even a sanctified amiability in the form of Christian meekness. Furthermore, it belongs to the nature of a virtuous principle to extend the area of the special affections. It is not mere outward distress that draws forth the sympathies; the feeling now extends to the soul as *sinful* and *lost*. These are entirely new elements. The natural man will feel deeply for one who has been crushed and torn by a machine; but he will manifest the utmost indifference in regard to a ruined soul just ready to plunge into a hopeless eternity. A benevolent principle superadded to the instincts of nature enables one to take in the whole of man, the soul as well as the body. In fact, the whole of being is enlarged. Man is carried into a new and higher region. The holy, the divine, and the eternal, he sees all around him. A new channel is made for the sympathies to flow in; a new force is added to the soul; a new character is given to the heart.

"Hence in estimating the precise moral quality of any beneficence, which man may have executed, it is indispensable to know in how far he was schooled into it at the bidding of principle, and in how far urged forward to it by the impulse of a special affection. To do good to another because he feels that he ought, is an essentially distinct exhibition from doing the same good by the force of parental love, or of an instinctive and spontaneous compassion—as distinct as the strength of a constitutionally implanted desire is from the sense of a morally incumbent obligation. In as far as I am prompted to the relief of distress by a movement of natural pity—in so far less is left for virtue to do. In as far as I am restrained from the outbreakings of an anger which tumultuates within, by the dread of a counter-resentment and retaliation from without—in so far virtue has less to resist. It is thus that the special affections may at once lighten the tasks and lessen the temptations of virtue;

and, whether in the way of help at one time or of defence at another, may save the very existence of a principle, which in its own unaided frailty, might, among the rude conflicts of life, have else been overborne. It is perhaps indispensable to the very being of virtue among men, that, by means of the special affections, a certain force of inclination has been superadded to the force of principle—we doubt not in proportions of highest wisdom, of most exquisite skill and delicacy. But still the strength of the one must be deducted, in computing the real amount and strength of the other; and so the special affections of our nature not only subserve a purpose in time, but are of essential and intimate effect in the processes of our moral preparation, and will eventually tell on the high retributions of eternity."*

We must not fail to notice this, however, that our sinful nature very frequently gives a coloring and direction to our constitutional affections, which really changes the instinctive benevolence into supreme selfishness. The love of country, for instance, very easily merges into vain glory. In the feeling of honor there may be pride. And even in the

* Chalmers, Moral Phil. p. 315.

case of sympathy, when one plunges into the water to save a drowning man, there may be a large share of self-glorification. In the family affections there may be idolatry,—loving children and one another more than God. Thus in many cases, no doubt, where persons have been praised for the performance of noble deeds, there have been out of sight the ever-willing impulses of a sinful nature. If men were sufficiently honest to make known their *motives*, much that is called benevolence would receive the proper name of sin. "Sin proceeding from the *will* as the primitive ground of all personal being, penetrates deeply into human development, entwines itself as a deadly creeper in all directions and ramifications of the same, everywhere checking, disturbing, and complicating. No sphere shows us any longer its true order in undisturbed form; as sin to the will, so error attaches to thought, impurity to the fancy, unhappiness to the feeling, and pain and sickness to physical life." * This being the case, natural goodness is greatly corrupted by moral evil. We do not see it in its purity, except on very rare occasions. Of course there are times, when man, prompted

* Müller, Doct. of Sin, vol. i, p. 411.

by his natural affections, performs deeds that are unselfish. A mother is quite likely to be disinterested when she leaps down a well to save her child. A poor outcast individual whom we once assisted will with the freest gratitude give us a cup of cold water which we may have asked from him. Such cases of unselfishness we admit. But really they do not destroy the fact of the total depravity of man. If man were unselfish because of a principle of love to God in his heart, then, we should say, he is not totally depraved; but when he is unselfish because a constitutional affection hurries him on in that direction, we cannot attach much moral importance to the fact.

The great evil with man is, that he is destitute of *holiness*. This he does not love. He desires not the spotless purity of God. Any amount of natural benevolence cannot make up for the absence of holiness. Instinctive goodness clings to man, just as the silver clings to the coffin that is rotting in the sepulchre. The thought presses upon us that there is a *lost feeling*. As we examine the mind of man, we perceive there every faculty of an intelligent being,—there is no lost faculty. But we do see that there is no central feeling of supreme love to God. There are many feelings suited to the different relations of life, but we cannot perceive one which unites the soul in holy love to the Deity. Here is the great evil. The one feeling that should give character to the whole man is lost; and so he is totally depraved. The inferior parts of the mind have, as a consequence, asserted the supremacy; and they rule as they please. Reason lifts up her voice, but her voice is not heard amid the din and turmoil of the passions. Conscience echoes forth the mandate of Heaven, but it is unheeded; right and retribution fail before the power of evil desire. The fire of the heart has gone out; and with the very ashes, the winds of appetite and selfishness have blinded the eyes of the soul. The electric spark has vanished away. There is nothing but a withered affection at the root of being. The great feeling is lost.

Thus we can see the absolute need of the supernatural. The life of God must again animate the soul. The lost feeling must be found. When the dead affection, which is sepulchred beneath the will, between the reason and the conscience, is again resuscitated, then an influence holy and divine will spread over the soul. A character then will be given to the special affections. They will be baptized with the power of the Divine Spirit. They will be set apart to a holy use. They will act for God, while acting for man.

It is possible that some one may endeavor to neutralize these statements by pointing to John Howard as the very personification of natural benevolence. That this great man had his share of natural benevolence, we feel willing enough to admit; but if he had nothing more, his whole career is a mystery. "The real Howard, who devoted his life to the jail and the lazaretto, was a very different person from that ideal of benevolence which the verse of Darwin, or the eloquence of Burke, had called up into our minds. Instead of this faint and classic ideal, we have the intensely and somewhat sternly religious man, guided and sustained, every step of his way, not alone, nor principally, by the amiable but vacillating sentiment which passes under the name of philanthropy, but by an exalted, severe, imperative sense of duty." "Those who have rested content (and we think there are many such) with that impression of Howard which is derived from the panegyrics scattered through our polite literature, and who accordingly attribute to him as the master motive of his conduct, simply a wide benevolence—a sentiment of humanity exalted to a passion—must be conscious of a certain uneasy sense of doubt, an involuntary scepticism; must feel that there is something here unexplained, or singularly exaggerated. Their Howard, if they should scrutinize their impression, is a quite anomalous person. No philanthropist they have ever heard of—no mere lover of his kind, sustained only by the bland sentiment of humanity, not even supported by any new enthusiastic faith in the perfectibility of the species—ever lived the life of this man, or passed through a tithe of his voluntary toils and sufferings." "The craving of his soul was some great task-work, to be done in the eye of Heaven. Not the love of man, nor the praise of man, but conscience, and to be a servant of the Most High, were his constant motive and desire."

To take from Christianity the honor of forming the great love of Howard, by holding forth this love as natural benevolence, is the highest species of spiritual plunder. The spring of Howard's philanthropy is made known to us in his own words: "The preparation of the heart is of God—prepare the heart, O God, of thy unworthy creature, and unto thee be all the glory through the boundless ages of eternity." We commend the life of such a man as a fine specimen of supernatural benevolence.

CHAPTER III.

SIN DEVELOPED, NOT HOLINESS, BY FIXED LAWS OF THE FEELINGS: THE SUPERNATURAL NEEDED TO GIVE A NEW DIRECTION TO THE HEART.

WE now turn our attention to a series of thoughts just the opposite of those which have been considered in the two previous chapters. Leaving the good, we come to the evil. If man is dead though possessing so much that is lovely, then is he twice dead by the sin that rages in the soul. There are laws of sin connected with man's emotional nature as fixed and uniform as the laws of the material universe.

1. *When one does wrong there is an attempt made to justify self.* Suppose a man has allowed himself to be wrought up to a very high degree of anger by reason of the remarks of another; the first tendency of the mind is towards self-justification. With all the conflict-

ing scene mentally present and the feelings still excited, the soul moves as quick as thought from point to point of the whole transaction, selecting the witnesses favorable to self and rejecting those that are unfavorable, by which means an apparently well-authenticated plea is established. If the man has any conscience at all, which we suppose he has, there will be a debate between that faculty and the feelings of the heart. There is really a doubt forcing itself on the attention, intimating that the late passion was not all right. The soul, however, is not willing to yield. Mental arguments derived from the reproduced scene are brought forward, and these in part silence the conscience. If the angry man is stubborn in his disposition, it will be all the harder to condemn self. He will stand up for his rights, and will naturally speak of the case to others if so be he may enlist them on his side. If he chances to meet one who witnessed the whole affair, and who joins in with him, this will be a great encouragement; he will now open his mind freely, mentioning at the same time the bad features apparent or real in the words and manner of his opponent. We may note also, that persons are more likely to justify themselves in habitual sins, than in occasional ones. Being habitual, they are loved more; hence it is not so easy to condemn self on account of them. Even the drunkard and gambler will advance arguments to uphold them in their wickedness. Yea, the murderer will tell you that through passion, revenge, or lack of money, he killed his neighbor, thinking by such a statement to palliate his crime. It is hard to confess guilt. The practice of making excuses, which is so common among mankind when they have done wrong, is the fruit of self-justification. Adam must needs blame Eve, and Eve the serpent; while it is possible that Satan justified his malignity by the fact that he was cast out of heaven. The last link in the chain is either to make God the author of sin, or to say that sin is a necessary ingredient of finite mind.

2. *Good feelings excited, but not acted out, increase depravity.* When one is prompted to duty by an impulse of the better nature, and does not heed this, but rather resists it, the holy spring or momentum is taken away. To every action or course of action there is feeling. This feeling is the motive power of the soul. Emotional energy is the strongest at the be-

ginning of a new course of life. More feeling is needed to start one on the path of duty than is needed afterwards, because benevolent habit is strengthened by every repeated act, and this takes the place of the feeling. Hence we speak of certain good men who act from principle, although they manifest no great amount of emotion, that not being needed so much as at the first. A duty by continual practice becomes easy, and demands less power; while at the first it was difficult, and demanded a great deal. Emotional force is thus saved, to be used for other duties about to begin, or other courses of action not fully established. Now, this wise arrangement is completely overturned when the excitation to duty is resisted. Even the idly wishing that we could do as the feeling dictates only hardens the sensibilities. Emotion also awakened by reading works of fiction, but not acted out, is deadening in its influence. The tears shed are not those that fall when one is seeking to elevate the wretched. This sympathy, which does nothing for the helpless and the vile, is but wasted pity, drinking the sacred life out of the heart. It turns men and women into lazy and weeping sentimentalists. They live and dream in an ideal world of existence, forgetting the actual scene of being that is around them with all its woes and wickedness. They would rather weep than work, rather sigh than save.

3. *Bad feelings are frequently awakened in the breast by the presentation of good objects.* This is a strange reversing of things; for the natural method is to present good objects in order to develop good feelings. The natural method, however, is overturned by a wicked heart. Suppose a benefactor suddenly to appear in our presence whose favors in times past we had not sufficiently esteemed,—we wish at once that he had not come near us. He only reminds us of our ingratitude, and thus arouses the conscience. Hence we treat him coldly, and wish him away. It is truly remarked by Kant, that "every benefactor ought to hold himself prepared for the awakening up of the propensity slumbering in the human heart to hold in aversion the object of its obligations." If the saying of the ancients be correct, that "nothing grows so soon old as gratitude," then, a sight of the man who befriended us must be distasteful to our feelings. The conduct of the Scribes and Pharisees towards the person of Christ forcibly illustrates the point. They

hated the truths which he uttered, although these truths were pure and holy; and they hated still more the pure and holy life which he exhibited. Hence to get him out of their sight they must needs kill him. It is a great mistake to suppose that all would love pure virtue if they could only once see it.

4. *A guilty man unwilling to do good is only irritated when his duty is pressed upon him.* There are two combined causes of this irritability. First, the man loves some sin or course of sin which he is unwilling to forsake, and so is displeased with any one who urges him to forsake it. Secondly, he feels guilty because of his wickedness; and, of course, the indignation of the moral faculty is only increased when a duty pointed out is not heeded. This complex state of mind tends greatly to sour the temper. One is frequently peevish and hasty without knowing the cause. The smallest matters will irritate a man when he is in this state. The greatest crimes will be committed when the light of truth and the fire of conscience surround and madden the spirit of the transgressor. The ocean foams the most when it breaks along the shore, and can go no further. Adam and Eve were never so miserable as

when the Lord God called them forth from their hiding place. The most wretched hour in the life of Judas was when he saw that he had betrayed the Innocent One. The torment of the wicked on a death-bed is caused by a vision of law and love.

5. *Sympathy in wickedness unites enemies.* Though to all appearance two persons must remain apart forever, inasmuch as they have no goodness to bring them together, yet not unfrequently they are brought to approve the same wicked deed, which at once makes them constant friends. The most noted illustration of this peculiar fact of mind is found in the conduct of Pilate and Herod with reference to Christ. These two rulers agreed in the act of condemning Jesus. Hence we read: "The same day Pilate and Herod were made friends together; for before they were at enmity between themselves." The subtle nature of this feeling in those who exercise it, doubless makes them think that it is a good affection that unites, and not an evil. But there is a diabolic harmony in the most unharmonious principle. Friendship because of sin, would never take place if sin were not loved.

6. *False zeal opposed or rendered unsuccessful*

turns to rage. A true feeling of enthusiasm will burn with more intensity when it comes in contact with opposition. Indeed, opposition seems to be a necessary condition for the development of a high and godlike enthusiasm. It is otherwise with the spurious feeling. Not being bottomed on truth and love, it is one-sided, and speedily ends in fury. Those wild persecutions, which have been undertaken by men inspired with a false zeal for the church, prove most conclusively the point before us. Such persons were only embittered and rendered perfectly furious by the unshrinking fidelity of the noble confessors of Jesus. No punishment was deemed too great for such obstinacy. Hence Neander speaks thus of one of the Roman emperors: "As the feelings of Julian against the Christians and against Christianity were continually more and more exasperated by the opposition which he experienced, it may be readily conjectured that, if he had returned back successfully from his Persian campaign, he would have become a violent persecutor of the church."* But all true zeal is patient. It never ends in bad temper. It is both pure and peaceable.

* Ch. Hist. vol. ii. p. 66.

7. *When one dislikes another, he takes pleasure in hearing the object of his dislike spoken against.* The eye brightens and the countenance glows as the faults of the hated man are circulated all around. The hatred appears to be consecrated by this means; there seems to be a ground for it; the pleasure therefore is great. If the kindred of the hated individual take also a dislike to him, this intensifies the joy. If any crime is discovered of which he has been guilty, this is fastened upon at once, and the profit added to the common stock. If any temporal evil befall him, as the loss of property, this produces a secret delight. The conviction is that he ought to suffer. This conviction may be kept a secret, as there is always more or less of sympathy for one who suffers loss; yet there is hidden gratification at the event. The element of revenge takes shape in the physical evil. The retaliation found in hatred is satisfied when the man suffers.

8. *When one hates another, it is natural to oppose his measures.* Hatred begets in the mind a feeling of prejudice against the person hated; and prejudice gives a false meaning to all that is done. Let even a good measure be

started by the hated man,—that makes but little difference,—it is natural to oppose. If certain persons, however, with whom the hater is on good terms, had made known to him the adopted measure, and had asked his coöperation without saying a word repecting its author, then, most assuredly he would have fallen in with it. But, if afterwards the author's name were revealed, the bitter opposer would now be troubled, and would wish to have no more to do with the scheme in hand. Every one can verify this picture by a little observation of men.

9. *If we would injure a person, it is natural first to blacken his character.* The mind with all its darkness and depravity still loves, at least, the appearance of consistency. It is hard to call the white black, unless we have thrown the dark shadow of our soul over it to make it appear such. If one must needs be condemned, he must first be found guilty. The Jews were eager to see Christ put to death; hence he who was holy was accused of blasphemy, and so nothing remained but to crucify him. If one would find a ground of objection against the Christian religion, it is enough to say that Christians are inconsistent, weak-

minded, and superstitious. When Gibbon would show the absurdity of Christianity, it seemed to him sufficient to state, "that the profane of every age have derided the furious contests which the difference of a single *diphthong* excited between the Homoousians and the Homoiousians."* A single diphthong might be a small matter to Mr. Gibbon when it related to the nature of the Son of God, and so good opportunity arises in making so much ado about it; but when the insertion of a small Greek letter in the middle of a word can change its meaning from the Infinite to the finite, all is different. Whether we have a system to condemn or a man to slander, evil of some kind must be associated with the disapproved object.

10. *A favor frequently bestowed, instead of producing gratitude, produces the feeling that one is entitled to receive the favor.* Let a beggar be in the habit of coming daily to your door in order to receive a portion of food. At first, he is grateful. After a season, however, he loses all sense of gratitude, and thinks that you are doing no more than right in supplying his wants. Should the usual gift cease, he will feel quite displeased, and will talk as if some

* "Decline and Fall of the Roman Empire," chap. xxi.

act of injustice had been done to him. It would seem that the act of beneficence, by being repeated, is viewed by the one benefitted as an act of justice, and being such, there is a claim to it. Perhaps the reason why the gifts of God make so little impression on the mind is the fact that they come to us so frequently. Hence the reason also why so few are thankful. Then, by and by, the hardened recipient will tell you that God is under obligation to take care of him, and that he, a sinner, is under no obligation to be thankful.

These are the laws of the feelings which have a bearing on the development of depravity. As facts of the existing nature of man they cannot be denied. We are led by them to take a more profound view of human sinfulness than is usually taken by the majority of men. These laws fix our attention on subjective depravity. We are led to look at inward states, rather than at outward acts. In the visible sphere, there may be a world of apparent goodness; in the invisible, a world of unmixed iniquity. Many are never conscious that they are averse to holiness; many never know that they are delighted with sin. How few, for instance, ever become cognizant of this fact—*that when one dislikes another there is pleasure in hearing the object of his dislike spoken against.* Yet this single characteristic lets us into the very secret of the heart's depravity. There is a real love of evil, and a certainty that that love will continue to show itself so long as man remains in his natural state. To speak of developing holiness is without meaning; sin only can be developed, as seen by the uniform working of the laws that we have pointed out. In fact, the whole moral nature may be said to be under one great law of sin and death. Self-reformation is morally impossible when this is the case.

Truth can do dothing to change the current and character of the soul. Indeed, if the truth is clearly perceived, it will arouse the evil of the heart, but will not lessen it or weaken it in the least. Suppose that a revelation of the unstained purity of God is flashed upon the mind,—will that wither and consume the moral evil that rages within the breast? Far from it. Just in proportion to the clearness and fulness of the vision of God, will be the strength of opposition against him. There can be no sympathy between a sinful nature and a holy nature. Evil will affiliate with evil, and will oppose the good. If the holy and perfect law of God is revealed to man, will it arrest his depravity? By no means. The law to a guilty man is more dreaded than anything else. The closer it is applied to the conscience, the more intensely is guilt aroused and enmity engendered. No truth, however high and however holy it may be, will sanctify and save a sinful spirit. If our design is to so shut up man that he will feel himself to be in a hopeless, helpless condition, no better method could be devised for the accomplishment of such an end than the simple presentation of divine truth. In this way there may be a preparation of soul for the supernatural, but nothing more. We admit, of course, that truth may develop an ethical life. All the outward movements may be well timed, pleasant to look upon, and instinct with favors to friend and foe; but what of all this, so long as the heart is dead. No man is right till he can say: "The law of the Spirit of life in Christ Jesus hath made me free from the law of sin and death."

Indeed, there is no security for any man except it be found in what may be called a *law of being*. The spiritual force or tendency of the soul must be in the direction of holiness and God. A man's chief end springs from the leading drift of the soul. A law of being is therefore the first and fundamental thing. Man must have a holy nature, if he would have an ultimate end that is holy. This is simply saying that he must be a law unto himself. Outward restraints are very good, for they may check the evil that is within to a certain extent; yet, if the evil is to be destroyed, the nature must first be changed. God acts as he does because of his moral being. The law that is to guide him forever is but the accepted law of his perfect nature. All is easy when this is the case. Even the good man thinks not of the law of the state. The divine movement of his soul is a law, and he needs no other. All the individual laws of the feelings that we have sketched will continue to be wrong, until the character of the soul is changed; for they are but so many movements of that character. The laws of the feelings as found in the angel mind do not mark the course of sin, but rather the course of holiness. A moral revolution in the character of man is therefore necessary if he would act like higher powers.

CHAPTER IV.

THE SOUL IN RUINS: A SUPERNATURAL RESTORATION REQUIRED.

THE soul in ruins! The very sound of the words produces sadness. We seem to be sitting in the midst of some of the fallen cities of the Orient. The oppressive sense of desolation breeds melancholy. We naturally bow the head and meditate. If a correct view would be gained of the ruins of the soul, we must take different stand-points. I begin, therefore, first, with the strife and conflict of the mental powers, as sure evidences of ruin within.

Conscience and the *heart* are at variance. Man can never sink so low as to lose the moral faculty. Without this there would be no ground of appeal. To restore man would require a physical miracle, if he had no con science. This great faculty testifies of God, righteousness, judgment. The peculiarity of the schism is, that the conscience claims supreme obedience, while the heart will not yield this. The *ought* of the one faculty clashes with the *aversion* of the other. Malice, envy, pride, ambition, selfishness, are in conflict with their opposites. Not only sinful acts, but sinful states, oppose the superior behests of conscience. This schism in the soul is felt all the keener when conscience is fully enlightened. Then the command is more imperative, and the opposition to it more determined. At the point when one would do good, evil is the most rampant. It is also a thought worthy of attention that, when a man is about to adopt a new and better course of life, then is the time that it is found to be the hardest. All the principles of evil marshal themselves together in an instant in order to oppose the good course, and to hold their own usurped supremacy. If one is about to adopt the Christian religion, he will find just at the turning point a mountain to ascend higher than ever appeared before. From the very nature of excited depravity there is a cross to be taken up. Not knowing this, many give way when they have almost reached the dividing line. Pride, enmity, and self-ease are all excited; and the soul falters. Each one must kill a Goliath before he can be the King's son. When a man is intimidated by the difficulties which the heart has called into being, the accusations of conscience break forth with full force, and the human spirit is rent in pieces. Remorse and condemnation worry the soul; secret hate and self-will tear the wound open which they have made. The enginery of conscience is fearfully at work beating against the walls of the spirit, making openings here and there; while the evil principles of the heart are digging down out of sight, undermining the whole.

Conscience is also opposed by the *propensities* and *appetites.* Neither the propensities nor the appetites are wrong in themselves. They belong to our original nature, and were designed for good. Yet the fact that they have an impulse which clamors for satisfaction shows us there is danger. And we know sufficiently well that they have gone beyond their legitimate use. Curiosity, imitation, the possessory principle, desire of esteem, emulation, the love of power, and other natural characteristics, have all gone into the region of selfishness. Conscience has not been able to keep these propensities in their proper place. Whether they first brought evil into the heart, or the heart first brought evil into them, it really makes no difference; now the whole soul is corrupted; and an evil influence goes from one realm to the other. The appetites, also, from their strong native power, have generally led captive the moral faculty. Man has become the sport and prey of his passions. There is a tendency to animalism. An immortal being is compelled to ride on the back of his lusts. Let the divine eye of the soul now be all light, and there is at once a war desperate in proportion to the might of the opposing forces. The stronger the attachment to evil, the fiercer the tumult within. This is in accordance with the law of every principle good or bad in the universe. *Each principle seeks to bring all into conformity with itself.* Hence, in the soul of man, each principle is a centre of attraction. Each acts according to its nature. Each would be victorious. This is the true reason of a schism in the human soul. There is a tendency in the good to draw all to goodness, and to repel the evil: and there is a tendency in the evil to draw all to evil, and to repel the good. We have thus different potencies in the creaturely spirit, acting according to their necessary laws. Each in its nature is distinct and unchangeable; and so long as they remain as they are, there must be war and confusion.

Reason and the *will* clash. The human reason sides with truth, duty, God. Away back of the passions, heart, and understanding, we have the reason speaking the clearest and the loudest in favor of the good. Optimism is the natural language of the highest faculty of the soul. Themes which are forcing themselves on the attention are approved or condemned by the reason. The upshot of all thought is echoed forth by this noble faculty. The doctrine of final causes is the doctrine of the reason. It may be affirmed with a good degree of certainty that the celestial reason approves the divine revelations of the Bible; and if men would but follow the promptings of their higher nature, not a sceptic would be found. The will, however, is vitiated; it is fixed to evil. It is not a fit organ for the reason; will not carry out its behests; is in a state of servitude to the heart. At times, indeed, it is whipped by the conscience into the performance of some outward duty; but this is so soulless, and so much against its native preference, that it counts nothing when measured by a divine morality. The will is habituated to evil; and though the reason speak ever so clearly it will not obey. When two of the noblest faculties thus run counter to each other, we can see what a tumult there must be within.

The intuition of the *divine* and the counterpart of this, *self-idolatry*, explain the jarring of the soul. The great battle of the ages is the conflict between God and the soul. All the other conflicts resolve themselves into this. The night-synthesis of depravity is *I.* All the atheism, pantheism, deism, and spiritualism, are merely attempts to elevate self at the expense of the Eternal. The great schism in the soul of man, occasioned by the divine and undivine, is but a type of the greater schism found in the moral system of the universe. The perturbations that move the monarchy of God are but the oppositions of the finite to the Infinite. The war of centuries and systems; of heaven, hell, and earth; of angels, demons and men; of truth, love and sin,—is no other than a terrible strife between the creature and the Creator, between the subject and the Sovereign. The soul is a little world with reference to moral anarchy, as well as with reference to other things. We behold the schism in all its malignity when we see the human asserting its supremacy over the divine. We wonder not now at the misery of man. The soul never can be happy without God. The flashing forth of the divine purity on the dark character of man must of itself make him utterly miserable. He may plunge deeper and still deeper into night, in order to get away from this and to feel easy in his mind; but the divine apparition will fail not to chase him, and at unexpected moments get before him, and look his soul into complete terror and dismay. One at some quiet hour may be complacently adoring himself; but in an instant God appears, and a mental tumult is the result. Like a thief caught in the act of stealing, or a murderer in the act of killing, so is it with man when God surrounds him in the midst of his wickedness.

Again, *unsatisfied aspirations*, even though *present good is obtained*, reveal a world of misery in the soul. Who does not know and who does not feel that even when all the good of time has been gained, there yet is restlessness and torment? This phase of the subject is indeed the most patent of any of the thoughts just mentioned. We come nearer in this to the consciousness of each individual. Much of effort is put forth to keep the soul easy. Anything is deemed better than realizing the gnawing pain of the human spirit. There is manifestly an attempt to get beyond the unhappy sounds of the soul. Excitement of some kind is generally found the most favorable. This drowns the plaintive cry of the troubled mind. It brings a glow over the soul. It is a species of mental intoxication. When one round of excitement is run, another must follow, or else the soul will begin telling of its misery. In this way life is passed, by the most of men. Few are willing to face the utter unhappiness of an immortal soul. Few are willing to meditate on their misery in order to comprehend and feel it, that they may the more earnestly long for a sufficient remedy. To forget the whole or a part is the more common way. Men flee from themselves as from a demon, that they may reach some angel good beyond them; and they are only willing to return when they have a bribe in their hand wherewith they may purchase peace, if it be but for an hour. How deep the aspirations of a human soul for something which the present can never furnish! "It thirsts after a good, invisible, immaterial, and immortal, to the enjoyment whereof the ministry of a body is so far from being necessary that it feels itself shut up and confined by that to which it is now united, as by a partition wall, and groans under the pressure of it. And those souls that are quite insensible of this thirst, are certainly buried in the body, as in the carcass of an impure hog; nor have they so entirely divested themselves of this appetite we have mentioned, nor can they possibly so divest themselves of it, as not to feel it severely, to their great misery, sooner or later, either when they awake out of their lethargy within the body, or when they are obliged to leave it."*

Still further, *sin is contrary to the constitution of the soul;* hence the misery which is ever felt there. If sin were in perfect harmony with the nature of mind, there could be no unhappiness; but now since there is unhappiness, we can only conclude that sin is a principle at war with the soul as God made it. In all the unrest of the spirit of man, we can see nothing but a protest against iniquity. Sin, although it has made a lodgment in the soul, is not there by the assent of the whole mind. There are voices ever and anon speaking against it. We know that sin has gained the heart and

* Leighton's Works, i. p. 657.

the will; and, so far as these are concerned, there is death-like harmony; but there is a deeper heart and a deeper will in the original native soul, both of which testify, though to no purpose, against its usurpations. In a profound sense, the soul is *duothelitic* instead of *monothelitic*. And in a sense equally pregnant with meaning, sin is *involuntary* as well as *voluntary*. The aboriginal soul, which is crushed down by the superincumbent mass of the developed one, will not acquiesce in sin,—here it is involuntary; while the developed soul does acquiesce,—here it is voluntary. There is a primitive spectral soul ever haunting the one that has wandered astray, and ever pronouncing a condemnation against its deeds of wickedness. No sin can reach this haunting spirit, neither can any misery frighten it away; it will follow after the wicked forever, and forever will it mirror forth to the descending soul the primal man. He that has gone deep enough into his being, beneath all his opinions and reasonings and logic ending in sin, must have noticed the utterances of a superior soul, telling of the pure, the divine, the endless; and never for a moment taking sides with the false or the sinful. Why the continual longing for something higher and better than earth can give, if sin be not against the constitution of the soul? Why guilt, punishment, and fear with its prophetic eyes, if sin be not an encroachment? The truth is, sin is a usurper; a despot reigns within. The soul recoils from its enemy. It will condemn the tyrant. It will approve the good. It will ever sigh and weep in its slavery. The soul in its deepest degradation will still cry for its God. It will not, it cannot, be at rest without him. Man was made for happiness, holiness, God; not for misery, sin, self.

All of these conflicting movements of the soul show its ruin. I proceed no further in this direction. A second stand-point, different from the preceding one, will now be taken, from which the wide spreading ruins of the spirit will be distinctly seen.

The *globe* which we inhabit first attracts our attention. There is much of beauty and fitness seen all around. The air, sea, and clouds speak volumes. The seasons tell their story of love. Continual food for the populous world is a miracle; continual drink for all is another. Wood, coal, and iron,—how much they speak of life, comfort and civilization. The very shaping of the earth shows wonderful adaptation. But there is another side. What mean the wild blasts that sweep with harshness? How bitter and cheerless the night of storms. The air at times is filled with poison and plague. The very sun burns up the fruit of the industrious. The worm gnaws out the life of vegetation. The sea arises in anger and breaks in pieces the mightiest ships. Myriads in agony sink in the deep. The earthquake overturns the scattered villages, and the inhabitants are devoured. The volcano sends forth a river of fire, and the cities are destroyed. What does this mean? Is the earth a paradise? Certainly not. No one can view the great house of mankind without feeling that the ruin there is typical. Something is wrong. We should not expect a perfect race of beings in such a strangely conditioned world.

The human *body* also shows symptoms of dissolution. Weakness stares us in the face. The pale countenance, the glassy eye, the wrinkled brow, affirm that something is wrong. Disease in all its manifold forms announces decay. Weariness and pain show that physical evil is at work. The house of the soul shakes under the force of the tempest. The rafters rot and give way. The roof sinks in. The building falls to the ground. Death proclaims corruption. That men die is enough. Why do intelligent beings come and disappear so strangely? Not merely the old man at the end of his days of weakness, but the youth. Even the infant has just time to weep, to look around,—then it dies. The very beasts suffer and expire. What says reason to all this? Does not the outward state of things impressively adumbrate some mighty catastrophe in the region of mind? Yes: the shadow of souls darkens all the earth.

But look at the *strange conduct* of our species. Here is a man all intellect,—no conscience and no heart. He can study creation without seeing God; he can study history and see nothing but man. Man has descended from an animal, the animal from an infinitesimal monad, the monad from a primitive ocean; that ocean is the mother of us all. Life has sprung from non-life; and death is an eternal sleep. Here is another man severing the head of a human being from the body, and then drinking the blood. His children are dashed on the ground; his mother is killed through kindness. There is a man worshipping a fly instead of the infinite God. There is another making a god;

and having finished his work, he prays to the wood. Here is one living a beggar, yet dying in the midst of abundance. We behold art and poetry also in their highest perfection, along with the deepest licentiousness. Science and sin are brought strangely together. Here are prisons with their criminals, fields of battle with their soldiers, and the greater part of the human family finding their chief good in the present life. But it is useless to continue. Any man can see that something is radically wrong. A view of the race shows that some mental and moral disaster has taken place.

How the ruin of the soul is apparent also from the *imperfect conceptions respecting human destiny.* "When I behold the whole universe silent, and man without instruction, left alone, and, as it were, a lost wanderer in this corner of creation, without knowing who placed him here, what he came to do, or what becomes of him at death, I am alarmed as a man is, who has been carried during his sleep, to a desolate and gloomy island, and who has awaked, and discovered that he knows not where he is, and that he has no means of escape. I wonder how any one can avoid despair, at the considereration of this wretched state. I see others around me having the same nature; I ask them if they know more on this subject than I, and they answer, no; and I see that these wretched wanderers, having looked around them, and discovered certain pleasurable objects, have given themselves up to them without reserve. For myself, I cannot rest contented with such pleasures, nor find repose in the society of beings similar to myself, wretched and powerless as myself. I see that they cannot help me to die; I must die alone; it becomes me then to act as if I were alone."* The human spirit is obviously in the midst of an eclipse. The Lofty One who reigns on high, the way of approach to him for sinful men, the quieting of the troubled mind, and the destinations of the future are themes which are not distinctly known.

The fallen soul is like a mirror cracked and broken. It does not reflect with truthfulness the image of the Deity. Like a watch out of order is the mind of man. It does not keep time with the clock of eternity. Changing the figure, we may use the words of John Howe: "Look upon the fragments of that curious sculpture which once adorned the palace of that great king; the relics of common notions; the

* Pascal, "Thoughts," p. 228.

lively prints of some undefaced truth; the fair ideas of things; the yet legible precepts that relate to practice. Behold! with what accuracy the broken pieces show these to have been engraven by the finger of God, and how they now lie torn and scattered, one in this dark corner, another in that, buried in heaps of dirt and rubbish! There is not now a system, an entire table of coherent truths to be found, or a frame of holiness, but some shivered parcels. And if any, with great toil and labor, apply themselves to draw out here one piece, and there another, and set them together, they serve rather to show how exquisite the divine workmanship was in the original composition, than for present use to the excellent purposes for which the whole was first designed."*

The soul, in fact, is like a palace all in ruins. Some of the pillars are fallen down and are broken, and others are standing erect as at the first. The once beautiful arches have given way, and the stones lie scattered all around. The bas-reliefs are defaced and full of holes. The decorated chambers are dingy, and the walls here and there have fallen in. The ceiling is damp, and the water dripping through, and descending

* "Living Temple," part ii, chap. iv.

to the floor. In the corners the mould has gathered, and an unpleasant odor infests the air. But there are some apartments mostly free from decay, and statuary is found but little corroded by the tooth of time. In different places, the hieroglyphics can still be deciphered, and inscriptions in the primitive languages be understood. It is very strange, too, that at the entrance of this once noble edifice we meet with two human-headed lions; evidently symbolizing strength, courage, and intellect. And it has even been said that the name of the architect has been found on a block in the great hall, though covered over by a stone on which was engraved the name of the original monarch who inhabited the building. Indeed, the whole fabric is a marvel; for some things are preserved as it were intentionally, while others are strewed around in great confusion. We may very properly apply to the whole the words of Layard: "The ruins were evidently those of a palace of great extent and magnificence. From the size of the slabs and the number of the figures, the walls, when entire and painted, as they no doubt originally were, must have been of considerable beauty, and the dimensions of the chambers must have added greatly to the general effect."*

Contemplating man as thus ruined, it cannot be an easy task to restore him. That preternatural aid is demanded for the restoration of the human spirit, may be seen from *analogy*. Consequently I here introduce some closing thoughts from this source to show the utter inefficiency of mere human power.

Here is a beautiful likeness of a friend, who has been dead for many years. It is the only one in existence; and consequently is prized all the more on this account. In a moment, however, it is broken into a thousand fragments. This creates deep sorrow; yet whatever the state of mind, there is no power to restore the likeness to its original condition. Here is a house burning with great fury. No one can quench the flames. They extend to the neighboring buildings, causing them to take fire. In course of time hundreds of noble mansions are consumed to ashes. And all this, too, with human power doing its best. What a symbol this of the ruin of souls! The smallest spark from a fire may have begun the work of destruction; yet small as the cause may be,

* "Nineveh and its Remains," vol. ii, p. 111.

the result is fearful. Here is an ocean steamer hastening to reach the port that is before it. Six hundred human beings are committed to its care. In an instant the ship is all in a blaze. Many are suffocated by the smoke; many are burned to death; many are drowned. And yet even this was caused by an accident. There was no design to destroy the vessel, far less the men who were in it. Still, even with an accident, an evil was started which no one could arrest. Hundreds perished; powerless they died; neither wish nor will saved them. So I may have power to shatter the image of the Deity; I may be able to introduce a destructive principle into the soul; and even by accident or unconscious influence lead others astray; yet I can neither stay the evil in myself, nor in the men whose ruin I have occasioned.

A wise man will not even think it safe to trust to himself when the mortal part is diseased, but will call in the best medical help he can find; surely, then, it must be the height of folly to profess to be the independent physician of the immortal nature,—a nature made in the image of God. Inasmuch as there are many diseases of the body which set at defiance all power of man or medicine, it is not at all strange that there should be one disease of the soul which baffles all the skill of human philosophy. It is true that I may have power to improve my spirit in many respects, just as I have power to regain the health of my body up to a certain limit; but this does not make it certain that I can restore my fallen nature in every one of its complicated and secret movements. I may so bridle my tongue that neither swearing, slander, nor lying, shall ever be heard by any mortal; yet, because I can do such things, it follows not that I can destroy the hidden evil of the heart. There is a consumption of the body which no man can cure; there is a consumption of the soul more deadly in its nature. It is quite clear that no man knows certainly that he is able to stop the reign of moral evil; for up to this time, no one is conscious of having done it.

Attention is now called to the fact of *death*. All men die. All have died since the beginning of time. Why is this? Why does life continue its movements up to a certain point, and then cease? Strange that no friend of the race should have discovered a remedy for this universal evil! It is quite likely that many would not even confess to a defeat here, unless compelled to it: yet the healers of souls have to die like other men. It is certain that an element of decay is found in each human body, which in a period of longer or shorter duration compels the principle of life to yield to its power. However much the two forces may struggle for the mastery, there is the dread certainty that the principle of death will at last be victorious. Now, since this is the condition of men as to their bodies, there is a very strong probability that an element of evil exists in their souls, and that this element of evil will outwit the highest wisdom of the creatures thus situated. In the universal reign of death, I see plainly the dark shadow of moral death; and as no man can overcome the one, neither is it reasonable to suppose that any can overcome the other. If one cannot destroy the lesser evil, most certainly he cannot destroy the greater. It would appear, therefore, that the principle of death in spirits must continue to operate forever; for as the soul is made in the image of the Eternal, even so through ages measureless it must continue its flight; yet with crippled wing and diseased heart ever departing and ever descending farther and farther from the perfect God. "Man can have no more right to expect that the soul's life can be renewed when it has been lost, than that he can restore health or life to the body after he has destroyed it by dissolute courses, or by his wilful act. Reason concurs with Scripture, that he may break the harmony of the divine creation, but can not renew it; that he may wander from God at his will, but can not return when he may please, and needs supernatural aid for the restoration of his spiritual life, no less than for the commencement of existence, or to call back a Lazarus from the grave."*

* Thompson's "Christian Theism," p. 403.

CHAPTER V.

NEED OF REDEMPTION: THE SUPERNATURAL REMEDY FOUND.

It is proposed in the present chapter to mention the different stages relating to the feeling of need. That the topic may be as distinctly marked as possible, I will begin where all is hopeless and end where all is hopeful.

1. There are periods in the life of man when *no need of redemption is felt*. Conscience has a night; then it sleeps. Not meaning by this that the sleep is sound and dreamless, for there are manifestations to the contrary. At intervals during the night, conscience trembles, groans, looks prophetically ahead. Then assuming a new position, it wants rest; is still; is locked in slumber. Says Archbishop Leighton: "The impenitent sinner is as one buried in sleep: his soul is in darkness, fit for sleep, and loves to be so. That he may sleep the sounder, he shuts all the passages of light, as enemies to his rest, and so, by close windows

and curtains, makes an artificial night to himself within: not a beam appears there, though without the clear day of the gospel shines round about him. The senses of his soul, as we may call them, are all bound up, and are not *exercised to discern good and evil.* And his leading faculty, his understanding, is surcharged with sleepy vapors, that arise incessantly from the inferior part of his soul, his perverse affections. Nor hath his mind any other exercise, in his sleepy condition, than the vain business of dreaming. His most refined and wisest thoughts are but mere extravagancies from man's due end, and his greatest contentments nothing but golden dreams. Yet he is serious in them, and no wonder; for who can discern the folly of his own dream till he is awake? He that dreams he eateth, when he awakes, finds *his soul empty*, and not till then."* The dead soul abides in a region of shadows, somewhat similar to Plato's dark cave. The real is not seen, but the unreal. Obligation is scarcely felt. Good is not seen as good, nor evil as evil. The individual who has sunk into this state, wonders at the solicitude of other men touching a way of recovery. He thinks

* Works, i, p. 456.

this to be nothing but the weakness of nature and the consequence of a bad education. As for himself he has not much trouble. A specious and external morality satisfies the feeble demands of the soul. He is even proud of his goodness; feels himself to be better than many who exhibit the graces of piety. Thus he is alive without the law; and redemption is not needed.

2. A sense of want is generated by the *changeable events of life*. There are but few men who begin and end the period of their pilgrimage with the same feelings. Time is too prolific of changes for that. One may be on the pinnacle of honor to-day, receiving the plaudits of an excited multitude; while to-morrow, he may be despised and cast down to the dust. A man may ride in his chariot of wealth at one time, with fictitious friends ready to flatter and submissive menials ready to serve; while at another, he may be forsaken of all. Adversity and prosperity form distinct chapters in the life of mortals. The clear morning terminates in the cloudy noon: the evening is dark and stormy. The soul has its seasons as well as the year; summer does not reach from the cradle to the grave. Sickness, be-

reavement, and sorrow are the triple heritage of man. Such things tend to bring the human spirit to itself. There are hours when the soul communes with its wants and its woes, and when it heaves forth a sigh of which none takes cognizance but God. Man has stopping places along the path of life where he sits down, thinks, and wishes for a good which he has not. Most minds have a reaction. By the discipline of life a certain feeling of need is brought out. The feeble eye of the soul looks dimly around, if perchance it may light on that which can satisfy the craving within.

I would not call this feeling of need, developed under the ministry of this world's affairs, the true feeling. It is at best but the voice of *nature;* and if it should happen to fasten itself to redemption, this is done as conceiving that it might answer to fill the *void* of the soul, rather than as the means to remove its evil. There are many, it is true, who go no further than this in their longing after redemption; they have no more than a nature-want; and so they would chisel down redemption to meet this, and thus destroy forever its identity and significance. The great thing is to have a spiritual need. Unless the point under consideration is well guarded, there is danger of lapsing into mere sentimentalism.

3. The *higher philosophy* tends to produce in man a sense of want. The truth of this statement is quite apparent in the marked experience of Augustine. "A passage which he suddenly came across in the Hortensius of Cicero, treating of the worth and dignity of philosophy, made a strong impression on his mind. The higher wants of his spiritual and moral nature were in this way at once brought clearly before him. The true and the good at once filled his heart with an indescribable longing; he had presented to the inmost centre of his soul a supreme good, which appeared to him the only worthy object of human pursuit; while, on the other hand, whatever had, until now, occupied and pleased him, appeared but as vanity. But the ungodly impulses were still too strong in his fiery nature, to allow him to surrender himself wholly to the longing which from this moment took possession of his heart, and to withstand the charm of the vain objects which he would fain despise and shun. The conflict now began in his soul, which lasted through eleven years of his life." "During this inward struggle, the acquaintance which

he had gained, by means of Latin translations, with works relating to the Platonic and New-Platonic philosophy, proved of great service to him. He says himself, that they enkindled in his mind an incredible ardor. They addressed themselves to his religious consciousness. Nothing but a philosophy which addressed the heart,—a philosophy which coincided with the inward witness of a nature in man akin to the divine,—a philosophy which, at the same time, in its later form, contained so much that really or seemingly harmonized with the Christian truths implanted in his soul at an early age; —nothing but such a philosophy could have possessed such attractions for him in the then tone of his mind. Of great importance to him did the study of this philosophy prove, as a transition-point from scepticism to the clearly developed consciousness of an undeniable objective truth."*

Philosophy was also one of the agencies that touched the soul of Neander. "The Judaism in which he had been brought up could not satisfy him. He felt the need of a religious life. *That* offered him only dead, cold forms which had forgotten the truths and feelings

* Neander, Ch. Hist. vol ii. pp. 354, 355.

they once expressed. His classical studies made him acquainted with Plato and he became deeply interested in him. He found much in him which harmonized with his own intense nature. There is a reflective earnestness in the strugglings of that noble mind after the truth which stirred all the sympathies of the young Jew. Here was what he most painfully missed in the formal religion of his fathers, and he embraced the great philosopher as a friend who had read his soul. Plato is his idol and his perpetual watchword. He pores over that author night and day, and there are probably few who receive him so completely into the very sanctuary of the soul. But when the glow of his first love had passed away, he found that though Plato had read his wants, he had not satisfied them. The Spirit of God had now awakened within him a deeper want, which philosophy has no means to supply."*

Philosophy has its place; but it never can generate a true need of redemption. It may prepare the mind in various ways for the Christian salvation; but it cannot lead man to accept of the divine Redeemer. Philosophy has a tendency, if rightly studied, to make the

* Biblioth. Sacra, vol. viii. p. 386.

soul dissatisfied with the limited and the temporal; it can intensify those aspirations which are oftentimes wandering hither and thither in search of an infinite good; it can increase the strife of the moral nature by the light which it sheds there; and by the enlargement of spirit which it creates, it can make man groan within himself as one shut up in a prison: but it never can snap asunder the chain, nor open the door of liberty to the captive. The great value of philosophy consists in this, that it makes man see how utterly powerless it is to do away with sin and misery. Its value is thus more negative than positive.

4. The need of redemption is developed in the truest manner by the *divine law* as *applied by the Divine Spirit*. All sin is against law; hence law is the true revealer of it, and the true antecedent of salvation. The following mental process may be noted: *a*. The law makes a man feel his obligation. It was seen under the first division that certain persons felt no need of redemption, because moral responsibility rested but lightly upon them. The legitimate effect of law is the arousing of conscience, and the extending of the mental vision in relation to good and evil. Man feels now

that he must act for the future; he feels also that he has not acted in the past. The law places the life and the character in a new light. Man like a soldier who has been sleeping on his watch is awaked by the word of command, and begins to act, and that with more faithfulness, seeing he has been unfaithful. *b*. Though the conscience prompts to right action, yet the incessant demands of the law make the man act wrong by stirring up the depravity of the heart. "The law is not sin, but it first renders the sin of the carnal tendency, which was dead and unconscious, actual, conscious sin, and represents it as universally sinful; that is to say, as worthy of death; and whilst it begets a knowledge of sin, at the same time effecting a more active or passive satisfaction in good, it can create a longing for redemption, and testify of its future realization."* The thought before us is one of the marked features in the Pauline development of sin as found in the seventh chapter of Romans.—"Sin, taking occasion by the commandment, wrought in me all manner of concupiscence. For without the law sin was dead." Man though convinced of his duty by his *conscience*, and though he may

* Nitzsch, "System of Christian Doct." p. 224.

attempt to do it, yet he is unwilling in his *heart;* that rises up against the purity and requirements of the law. *c.* The sinner now is conscious of a schism in the soul. Aversion to what is good becomes apparent. Two forces are struggling the one with the other. The evil always prevails. The man sees and feels this. His heart sinks, and his soul trembles. *d.* All hope of being saved by the law is now lost. The former works in which the soul trusted are swept away. They are rent in pieces like the light sails of a ship in a hurricane. The soul is tossed by the waves, with no prospect of reaching the land in safety. Self-righteousness is gone. "By the deeds of the law no flesh shall be justified." A healthy conviction of sin is now the result. The soul says, "I was alive without the law once: but when the commandment came, sin revived and I died." What can the man do? He can do nothing but sin. He is lost out and out. He is driven almost to despair. *e.* With the aid of the Spirit he longs earnestly for redemption. He prays for help and pardon. He would be saved from sin and its consequences.

5. The need of redemption as thus developed leads the sinner to the Saviour. The understanding now is enlightened and satisfied; the

conscience is directed and quieted: the heart is changed and made to centre upon God; the will is liberated and set for holiness. I will not say that every one who comes to Christ has the very experience that has been mentioned above. There are a vast variety of minds, and a vast variety of modes. One is converted in this way, and another in that. Tholuck makes the following judicious statement: "According to the diversity of natural dispositions will men be brought, at different periods, to a sense of the value of such a faith. One passes through the sharpest conflict at his first awakening; another in the season of base lukewarmness, which so frequently follows the first glow of love; a third is drawn to Jesus with feelings and views not strongly defined, and only after long intercourse with him learns to know his own corruption, and to rely firmly on the atonement, when he has already tasted somewhat of the Saviour's grace. This latter way God often chooses with minds of strong powers, but whose depravity is proportionably deep; who, if they had been made fully sensible of their own corruption before Christ had been manifested to them, would have sunk stupefied into the arms of despair. For this reason it is impossible to lay down any settled modes of conversion: the spirit of God 'bloweth where he listeth,' and as he listeth. Only earthly things are to be determined by line and measure; divine things are not *contrary to*, but *above* our line and measure. One pilgrim travels by the Isthmus of Suez: another goes through the Red Sea and the wilderness; but both reach the promised land."* It is supposed, however, that each has a view of *sin*, and a view of *law*, although the feelings with reference to these may differ as to *intensity*. It is morally impossible to accept of Christ while there is no consciousness of guilt. Whether one is led to the Saviour by the law or the gospel, by justice or mercy, or by the combined force of all redemptive agencies,—*the under-current of spiritual experience is essentially the same.* If one is converted in a storm, another in a calm, and another he knows not how,—the primal state of mind which leads to Jesus must possess the same inherent elements. There may be thousands of extraneous circumstances connected with the turning of souls, but the turning is one. There is but one salvation and but one faith. The ignorant savage and wise philosopher, the little

* "Guido and Julius," p. 180.

child and man of a century, repent of sin in the same way,—there is but one repentance. Still, though this be all admitted, the man who is brought to Christ by the ministry of law and sovereignty, possessing the most exalted views of God and his government, along with the deepest self-abasement because of sin,—such a man (other things being equal), must be the strongest Christian. He has been born in a bracing climate, and there is a tone to his health not found in others. He who has not passed through this kind of experience in the beginning of the new life, the sooner afterwards he does pass through it the better. No character is complete without a large infusion of the judicial element.

6. The soul in its pressure and want having found Christ, Christ is now the great *animating presence.* Man needs to be stimulated and lifted up. He needs a chief motive that is divine, and an inspiration that is divine. The cross with the God-man hanging thereon is the power. Church history mentions a striking incident connected with the life of Constantine. He was about to commence a war; and being at a loss to know to what deity he should apply for help, he concluded to betake himself to

the one Almighty God. Therefore, he applied, praying that he would reveal himself to him, and lend him the protection of his arm in the approaching contest. While thus praying, a short time after noon, he beheld, spread on the face of the heavens, a glittering cross, and above it the inscription: 'By this conquer.' The emperor and his whole army, now just about to commence their march towards Italy, were seized with awe. While Constantine was still pondering the import of this sign, night came on; and in a dream Christ appeared to him with the same symbol which he had seen in the heavens, and directed him to cause a banner to be prepared after the same pattern, and to use it as his protection against the power of the enemy. The emperor obeyed: he caused to be made, after the pattern he had seen, the resplendent banner of the cross."* This was carried forward in the presence of his soldiers as the inspiring symbol of victory. So when one is about to commence the moral battle of life, and is conscious of the need of help, the cross will ever nerve him with a power divine. The world has never seen such heroes as the soldiers of Christ. Never before

*Neander, Ch. Hist. vol. ii, p. 7.

has there been such electric feeling, fixedness of purpose, perseverance, as in the men of Jesus. *By this we conquer* is the motto, watchword, and hope of the good.

Chateaubriand, in one of his fine descriptions, speaks of two soldiers who were so united to each other by the bonds of friendship that they fastened themselves together by a chain on the field of battle, determined that their fate should be the same. "One had fallen dead beneath the arrow of a Cretan; the other, though struck with a mortal wound, was still alive, and reclining over his brother in arms. 'Warrior,' cried he, in a faint, expiring voice, 'thou hast fallen asleep after the fatigues of the battle. Thine eyes shall open no more at my call; but the chain of our friendship is not broken, it still links me firmly to thy side.' As he finished these words, the young Frank fell exhausted, and died embracing the body of his friend. Their beautiful locks intermingled as they fell, like the wavy flames of a double fire expiring on the altar, like the trembling rays of the constellation Gemini, where it sinks into the sea."* Christ and the Christian are fastened together. In the midst

* "The Martyrs," book vi

of the conflict they will not be separated. The stronger will animate the weaker: the weaker will trust in the stronger. When the man of earth falls, the Man of heaven will comfort his spirit. Reclining on the bosom of Immanuel, the dying saint and soldier ends life. His last words are—"Thanks to God, who giveth us the victory through our Lord Jesus Christ."

CHAPTER VI.

MAN ESTRANGED FROM GOD: THE PHILOSOPHY OF THE SUPERNATURAL CURE.

ESTRANGEMENT from God is the most elementary characteristic of depravity. We therefore commence with its analysis. By this means we shall be the better able to understand the nature of that change which must take place in the existing character of the soul.

1. The first movement of estrangement from God begins in a region *back of consciousness*. To some persons this idea may seem to be absurd. How, it may be asked, can there be such a thing as unconscious sin? It only wants a little attention, however, to see that our statement must be correct. Who can tell when he began to sin? Can any one give a true and faithful account of that fatal moment in his spiritual history when he took the first downward step to ruin and wretchedness? No: memory knows nothing about it; man knows nothing about it. The whole world have sinned, and yet not

one in the world can tell when first he sinned. It is not that the ignorant are thus situated; the wise are in the same condition. And this is not merely the state of those now living upon the earth, but the collective generations of time have all been in darkness touching the first sin. Whether any struggle took place during the primal fall, no one can inform us. Whether man saw the enemy and fought against him, or sank down at once, without a sigh, without a tear, is all unknown. Surely it is strange that the most significant sin of the entire race should commence in a sphere beyond consciousness. A word falls without knowing it! Man having begun in this way, it is quite likely that depravity will be mainly propagated in a stratum of being beneath the plane of conscious apprehension. The first movement of every leading fall of the soul is doubtless of an occult character. Each great fall is generic, and has connected with it a host of individual sins. Many of the individual sins may be known, but the chief sin that makes certain all the others is to a great extent unknown. Thus we have a world of iniquity in the soul involved in complete mystery.

2 Estrangement from God is a *state of mind.*

The miser loving his gold; the revengeful man hating his enemy; the worldling eager to drink every cup of human pleasure,—each has a specific state of mind characterized by the distinct evil. So much has been said in modern times about sin as an isolated act, that many have lost sight of the important fact that sin is also a permanent state. The main fault we find with the atomic view of sin is, that it is too superficial. No one will ever understand the true nature of his depravity until he plunges into the deep of the heart, and there discovers fixed opposition to all that is good. All the evil that a man does is but the result and outgrowth of the inward state. Character is chiefly found in this subjective condition of the soul. If sin and holiness were merely volitions, the man who had good volitions would be fitted for heaven, even though his heart were in a state of opposition to God and goodness. The vain-glorious desire, the envious feeling, the malicious thought, and spiritual indifference would then count nothing. Such a view of human sinfulness must be false. We are forced to believe in a movement of the will that is more profound and more comprehensive than that which is seen in mere volitions. There is a great choice of all choices. The collective depravity of the soul is encompassed and carried forward by the far-reaching power of the human will. It holds with the grasp of a demon the spirit of man. The will digs a channel for the pollution of the soul to flow in. The current of evil sweeps on ceaselessly as the hours, and fearfully as the march of death. This great transcendental sweep of the will had its commencement with the first sin of the individual. Since that first fall it has not ceased for a moment to act. It is all-embracing, constant, fixed. Yea, it is evermore increasing in power. The depraved state is strengthened by its own continued movement.

3. Estrangement from God implies *self-dependence*. As we go back in our mind to the sin of Adam, we see its dark advent in the withdrawing of the finite from the Infinite. Man holy had the most unshaken confidence in the perfect God. Through the agency of a most insinuating temptation he fell from the divine sphere. The shock startled him; his eyes were opened; God was gone. If one would ascertain the true nature of his sin, he has only to see that he does not depend in a spiritual manner on the Independent. There may be a

species of natural dependence, but this is destitute of holiness and love. There may even be an intellectual trusting, forced into existence by the power of truth, but it is cold, cheerless, unspiritual. The supernatural tie, which binds all good souls to God, binds not man to his Maker; it is snapped asunder; and now man is living in a cycle of being which is small, earthly, selfish. There is a loss of the consciousness of God. All good spirits abide in the midst of the ever-beaming presence of the Deity. They have a constant vision of God. But when sin begins, Jehovah disappears; the vision then is lost. Man now falls back on himself; and, as he has no Supreme Being to worship, he worships himself. Of course, it is not necessary that each one should sing a psalm and offer a prayer in order to deify self; the outward life is a psalm, and the inward life a prayer. "All unbelief in the true God, and his holy revelations, has ever some superstition for its never failing reverse side, if it be only the belief in the all-sufficiency of one's own critical and sceptical understanding: the departure of the Divine principle of life, is immediately connected with the arrival of a principle in opposition to the Divine. Man cannot dethrone the true God without putting an idol in his place."* There is now the negation of all good. Alienation and love cannot exist together. Even if we admit that there are smothered sparks of goodness in the soul of man, this can avail nothing so long as evil has the ascendency. If the tendency to sin is strong, constant, and increasing in its power, as facts everywhere show, then, latent goodness is only a pretty fancy, a kind of half-remembered dream of heaven, a shred of the royal robe of glory, a gem saved from the original catastrophe, which, by the contrast, only shows how universal and hopeless is the spirit's ruin. Because a monarch sinks in the depths of ocean with a crown on his head, the loss is none the less.

4. Estrangement from God is from its nature *eternal;* that is, left to itself, it must continue forever. Only let sin have a beginning, and that settles the matter for eternity. Let any being sin but *once,* and there is no return. It is a fundamental law of motion that a body set agoing will roll on forever, unless something come in its way to stop it. So is it a fundamental law of sin that once begun it must continue, unless some extrinsic power interfere to

* Müller, Doct. of Sin," vol. i, p. 133.

arrest it. If we can believe the former, we need not doubt the latter; for the physical truth is not more certain than the moral. No created being has lived forever to see either the law of motion or the law of sin certified; yet, there being sufficient evidence, the one may be as firmly believed as the other. Certain facts may be mentioned which seem to intimate that sin will be eternal.

A large number of the angels sinned in heaven. With their first sin they went down. We know that these fallen powers existed at the time of Christ; but no intimation is given that even one had ceased to do evil, although a period of at least four thousand years must have passed away since their first departure from God. Instead of ceasing to trample on the divine law during any portion of this period, they rather increased in their wickedness. Their condition thus became more hopeless during these four millenniums of rebellion. Add to this, that these same vicious powers are to continue their opposition to God throughout the whole history of time, and we have a course of sinning of vast extent. Beings who will sin from the creation to the end of the world will certainly sin forever. As far as we see the working of moral evil in this world, the same principle is apparent. During the long lives of the population before the flood, we behold nothing but the increase of wickedness. Men indeed became so bad that punishment had to burst forth upon them. At the close of the present dynasty, we are assured also that countless throngs of sinning men will come forth to be tried and condemned; thus making it certain that they have not reformed during their abode in the intermediate state.

Now, in seeking to discover a law for anything, we rest not short of uniformity. A grain of wheat will produce nothing but wheat; there is a uniformity here which never fails; and therefore we doubt not in regard to it. The planets have been careering through space ever since their creation, attracted always to one central sun; hence we see no reason to doubt the law of gravitation. And, surely, it is no more difficult to find the law of sin; for we have a uniformity as unvaried as the attraction of worlds. Seeing an apple fall from a tree suggested the law of gravitation; and so unwavering was the confidence in this that in a moment the law was applied to the whole of matter. In the same way we notice the fact of sin in the realm of mind, and at once announce the law which must continue so long as mind is left to its own native working.

It is worthy of attention also that the law of sin is double; that is, it goes from mind to mind, ever increasing in *extent* as well as in *duration*. Moral evil is not an isolated force; it cannot stay in the soul where first it began; it must spread from its very nature. To see a sinner living in the government of God without casting a blight upon other minds would be a moral wonder. To have no inclination to extend evil would be the highest proof that it did not exist. There is always a will to extend, whether that can be successfully carried out or not. This movement gives us the law of sin with reference to *space*, while the other gives us the law of sin with reference to *time*. We thus have a growth in opposite directions. And not only this, but in the diffusion of sin we have myriads upon myriads of distinct starting points from which it spreads out forever. It is not as if one being were to act by itself in eternal opposition to God, but millions are warring against Heaven. This exceedingly strengthens our argument for the endless nature of sin. Not by the mouth of two or three witnesses do we seek to establish the point, but by countless multitudes. And the testimony of all these individuals is doubled by the double law of sin before us. For while each one will sin by himself forever, each will also cast an evil influence over the other throughout the same eternity. Extension and duration are the warp and woof of sin. It is this twofold view which discloses the vastness of the evil that disturbs the universe of God. How mighty the consequences of one sin! We say *one* sin, for that reverses the whole working of mind. It is the one act that gives a bent to the soul, that excludes all taste for holiness, that leaves nothing but estrangement from God. One solitary sin has in it the destinies of eternity. It utters a fearful prophecy of the soul's downward way. Sin will torment souls forever; it will trample on the divine law forever; it will be the great anarchist of the universe forever; it will defy God forever.

With this fourfold view of estrangement, it is morally impossible for human nature to leap out of itself into a new spiritual state. If sin were a temporal evil, and not an eternal one, all would be different. If it were like the derangements of the solar system which, after a vast circle of ages, will pass away, bringing the whole back to harmony, then, we might say that a supernatural redemption is not needed. But this is not the case. The derangements caused by sin in the moral system of the universe do not resolve themselves ultimately into a scheme of eternal fitness and order. Man without redemption must continue in his course of evil. And no difference will it make if God should forgive sin, as some say he will, independently of the Christian remedy; for even admitting that he is so good, or so bad, as to forgive sin in this way, what still is to be done with man, for he will increase in sin forever? The pardon of sin does not remove the evil; and it is the removal of that which is the great want of the case. If pardoning all the criminals in the land would make them sinless men, no more could be desired. Here is the difficulty, and there is no use of shutting the eyes against it. Surely if any thought is of greater importance than another it is this—how shall I be delivered from sin? It is just at this point where scepticism fails. After destroying every vestige of the supernatural, the sceptic sits down with great joy on his countenance because of his boldness, not thinking that while he has taken away all, he has left nothing in its place. Plainly there is no priestcraft about sin. This is a fact of the race entirely independent of revealed religion; and the infidel must have courage to meet it. Tell how it can be banished from the soul; state the remedy in plain terms. If this cannot be done, be willing at least to contemplate the subject in a serious manner. To be indifferent respecting a matter so great as this, is neither wise nor manly; for the most profound intellects of all ages have been exercised with reference to this very problem.

If supernatural influence, then, is to change the existing depravity of the soul, in what way must it act? In what way must it begin? There must be a certain mode. The remedy, if it would be effectual, must be conditioned somewhat by the nature of the disease. As estrangement from God, therefore, is fourfold in its nature, so reconciliation to God must be fourfold also. The philosophy of restoration is but the antithesis of man's departure from the Deity. The nature of the disease shows what must be the nature of the cure. In the way that moral evil began in the soul, we have an intimation respecting the way that moral good must begin.

First, then, as the initial movement of sin in the race is back of consciousness, so the initial movement of divine life must be also back of consciousness. It is absolutely necessary that the supernatural should begin its heavenly work in the dark region of the soul. In no other way can the evil be reached; in no other way can it be rooted out. That man can do nothing here is plain. He cannot proceed to depths that are unfathomable. He can neither rout the invisible enemy, nor storm the invisible citadel. How is sin, then, ever to be destroyed? How is man ever to be made holy? He is forced to turn his attention to a Superior Power. The Spirit who knows human nature and human sinfulness in their totality can make his abode in that sphere which is out of sight; and there with a love, all the greater because it is not perceived, he can work at the very foundation of depravity; resting not till that foundation is undermined, the building that was erected upon it overturned, and a new one raised in its stead. The Restorer of souls may thus work among the principles of our depravity without at all infringing upon any of the laws of the mental nature. Yea, everything like undue pressure may be obviated all the more by the very fact, that the Spirit makes no direct assault upon any of the faculties, but is contented to touch the hidden springs that lie far beneath; and thus, moving them, he moves effectually the whole man. As sin has fixed its habitation in the very interior of the human spirit, I see not why God may not be acting there with as much safety and efficiency as among those powers whose ongoing is seen by the eye of the soul. If he would change the course of the wide and deep river, the most reasonable method is to begin with the streams that steal forth from the base of the mountain; and changing them, a new channel is made for the current to flow in. The rain which to-day waters our fields may have received its first movement earthward in the remotest region of the clouds; and the wind which now sweeps by us with all the force of a tempest may have been started on its course a thousand miles away; "The wind bloweth where it listeth, and thou hearest the sound thereof, but canst not tell whence it cometh, and whither it goeth: so is every one that is born of the Spirit." Whatever our theory may be, it is very certain that we know nothing *directly* of the Spirit as he works in the souls of men. We are only *conscious of certain results.* New emotions of love and joy attract our attention; a new faith exercised and a new life adopted make us to see that a work of grace has commenced in the heart.

Secondly, as estrangement from God is a state of mind,—a state surrounded by a mighty act of the will,—an act back of all individual volitions,—so now this active state must be changed, man must *repent.* Here our method harmonizes with the gospel method. The fundamental requirement that meets us in every book of the New Testament is just this: "Repent ye, and be converted, that your sins may be blotted out." "Except ye repent, ye shall all likewise perish." To turn about with the whole mind is what the Bible means by the act of repentance. There must be a great voluntary act, which comprehends within itself a holy and fixed state of mind. The man who confines transgression to mere volitions must, if he be consistent, consider himself as sinless during the interval that comes between the volitions. Sin in this way begins with every new act: very much in the same way that a holy being sins for the first time. Repentance according to this view would be nothing more than a mere isolated choice,—a choice which could have but little influence on the permanent character of the soul. A deeper and more radical change must take place than this. Leave man with his fixed state of mind, and it is impossible for him ever to reach holiness. The one voluntary act of sin, which encompasses the mind, must lose itself in one soul-felt determination to glorify God. When this is done, a vast number of subordinate purposes follow. A single holy choice may succeed the great soul-choice, but it cannot precede it. The lesser cannot generate the greater; it is enough if the greater move on to the production of the lesser.

It might seem as if we were swinging round the soul from a perfect state of sin to a perfect state of holiness, and yet this is not the case. When the predominant choice of self gives way to the predominant choice of God, it does not follow that all sin instantly departs from the soul. Hidden depravity still remains; and at points here and there bursts forth into open transgression. A purpose may be ultimate, but not perfect; hence ignorance, inattention, passions of various kinds, outward temptations, may lead the soul into sin. Yet we imperatively demand that the change in man be effected in his *ruling disposition.* It is just here that we see the weakness of mere natural development. There is no attempt made to turn the great moral current of the soul. Indeed, it were utter folly to attempt anything of this kind. The soul is pledged to sin by its own supreme act. The act is complete and total, leaving no balance of moral power to be used for self-restoration. How can the will turn against itself when thus situated? The captivity of the soul is voluntary; and consequently an all-embracing moral change is morally impossible. We may say truly with Coleridge, that there is a *nature* in the will. The voluntary faculty acts for sin with all the certainty and regularity of a law of nature. With this view of the subject, there is a perfection of wisdom manifested in the Christian method of repentance.

Thirdly, we said that estrangement implies self-dependence; therefore, if man would be saved from sin, he must depend on the divine Redeemer,—he must *believe.* This is the way to bring man back again to God. As all sin is anti-theistic, so there can be no divine life in the soul without a filial connection with the Divine Being. The lost confidence must be restored. What is faith? It is a heartfelt acceptance of Christ; it is a *soul-dependence* on the only Saviour. The entire human spirit lays hold of Jesus. Faith is not an isolated act of the mind. It is not the mere assent of the understanding; not the simple outgoing of the feelings; nor yet the individual movement of the will: but it is the collective act of the soul. Faith is thus the highest, holiest, grandest act of the spirit of man. The entire soul is conveyed over to Christ. The act of faith is, in fact, just the counterpart of the act of the atonement. The Redeemer yielded up his entire being as a sacrifice for the salvation of men, and so men yield up their entire being to him in order to obtain this salvation. Christ gave himself to die: man gives himself to live. The whole soul is thus an offering. There is nothing unreasonable in Christian faith; it is the very perfection of reason. The unreserved, unconditional, and total surrender of the soul to Christ, is a sublime act of devotion. There is not a mere belief in testimony, as this is too cold and impersonal; there is not a faith in Jesus as simply the great teacher, the model man, the martyr, for these are but human characteristics; but there is a soul-acceptance of the God-man. There is but one Saviour, and but one committal of the whole man to him for time and eternity. In this way, self-dependence is rooted out of the mind; and a holy confidence in the world's Deliverer takes its place. The Christian salvation thus restores man to his normal condition.

Finally, as estrangement from God is eternal in its nature, so reconciliation to God must be eternal. The gospel meets this demand. The rudiments of the higher life exist in the new nature of the Christian. The saintly man of heaven is seen in miniature in the converted man of earth. Through the agency of truth, providence, and grace, the supernatural germs develop themselves; and thus the man in Christ Jesus is made perfect. The Christian redemption would be a failure if eternal and fixed holiness were not its fruit. As souls, then, are purified and perfected, we can ask no more. Estrangement in its fourfold nature is destroyed by a fourfold restoration, culminating in a life endless and divine. The ruins of the fall are thus set aside. The condition of man primeval is again reached. A new kingdom of saved souls is to begin its eternal march. An innumerable company of godlike men are even to stand upon a higher platform than that of Adam in Paradise, and are to work out a more glorious destiny than he could attain to, because of their connection with the redemptive powers and forces of the Son of God. "Where sin abounded, grace has superabounded."

PART III.

Voices of the Soul answered in God the Satisfier.

CHAPTER I.

HINTS RESPECTING A NEBULOUS REGION IN THE SOUL, AND ITS RELATION TO THE FUTURE DEVELOPMENTS OF GOD.

ALL persons of a subjective tendency must be conscious of a region of clouds in the soul so strange and confused that all attempts at distinct apprehension seem to be unavailing. The most scrutinizing consciousness is only able to note down the fact of such a dim realm of being; the contents of the fact remaining out of the reach of the orb of vision. This nebulous sphere is as yet an unexplored territory. It is only seen in the dim distance, as one sees a new land through the gray mists of the dawn. Something is apprehended, but what that something is no one can tell. Perhaps, at some favorable moment, the attentive spectator may imagine that he beholds a moving to and fro like the shadows of clouds and birds in a lake, but just so sure as he stops awhile, in order to give form and distinctness to what he thinks he sees, all is gone.

He who has watched the working of the human mind along the path of history must have noticed the feature of indistinctness that we here refer to. The ancient mythology is a most striking instance of it. Poetry is full of it. In speculative philosophy we see it to a greater or less extent; and at different periods more than at others. The system of Plato has much of its attraction from the divine darkness that here and there gathers about it. The strange philosophies of the Orient could never have had an existence save as they were the outgrowth of vagueness mingled with a degree of distinctness. What could Gnosticism have done without its land of shadows? The Hindoo pantheism is but a bold attempt to penetrate the unknown. And the modern pantheism of Germany only shows how the mind struggles to give shape to the shapeless. In the sphere of theology and religion we have also the indistinct element. The mystics have always felt at home here. Even in superstition there is something which finds a basis in the gloom of souls.

That there is a dark zone in the mind of man must be admitted by all. How to explain it is not easy. A somewhat suggestive passage is found in Coleridge's article on the "Greek Drama," which may be quoted: "The Greeks," he says, "idolized the finite, and therefore were the masters of all grace, elegance, proportion, fancy, dignity, majesty—of whatever, in short, is capable of being definitely conveyed by defined forms or thoughts: the moderns revere the infinite, and affect the indefinite as a vehicle of the infinite;—hence their passions, their obscure hopes and fears, their wandering through the unknown, their grander moral feelings, their more august conception of man as man, their future rather than their past—in a word their sublimity."*

As a preparatory thought, we may note the *unconscious knowledge* that exists in the soul. At first, it seems to be a contradiction to say that the mind knows a thing, and yet is not conscious of knowing it. It must, however, be true. By the law of association a great part of mental action is carried forward; yet how very few of the links in the chain of association are we conscious of. It is only occasionally we notice one thing that has been suggested by another; the greater part is never consciously perceived. We are certain, how-

* Works, vol. iv, p. 29.

ever, that the mind itself must have perceived the various links in the chain ; for without such an act of perception, the suggestive process were impossible. There is flowing into the soul a perpetual stream of knowledge, which never comes within the range of either consciousness or memory. Sometimes the most astonishing revelations of latent wealth will dart forth while persons are in the midst of a high fever or in a state of insanity, showing that a power of mind has been at work in appropriating truth, secret and hidden in its nature. Even in sleep, persons have startled others by communications of knowledge which was not known to exist while awake. There is good reason to think that an extended kingdom exists in the mind shrouded in darkness, —greater even than the kingdom of light. Sometimes there is an attempt to penetrate the gloom. Nothing definite, however, is perceived. A more powerful instrument might open up the nebulous mass and resolve it into a glorious system, but under the present mundane development this is not to be expected.

It is probable also that the cloudy state of the soul arises, in part, from the *infancy of the soul* itself. We have just begun to exist. To a child there must be a great deal that is wholly indefinite. At first, nearly all is of this character. After a season, however, distinctness and certainty extend their area. But how small is the gain. Some things that are clear to the man are dark to the child; while again there are other things that are dark to both. Looking at man as an immortal being, he is now but an infant. Cradled between the two eternities, his head is almost hidden from view as it leans upon a pillow of clouds; only the lower part is seen to be skirted with the light that is everlasting.

Then, again, we must suppose that there are *germs and seeds of eternal ideas* in the human spirit. What man will be a thousand years hence is shadowed forth in the mind. The ideas that are just appearing are types of endless being. There are, no doubt, germs of truth in the mind which we can only half see by scraping away the soil that is about them; and which will not appear above ground till the spring-time of eternity draws near. There may even be certain ideas of the soul which have not yet dawned into conscious life, but are struggling to do so; and as a consequence of this, we think we hear certain whisperings or see certain motions, but all is so doubtful that we are compelled to let them go. Undiscovered thoughts must therefore form intangible states of mind.

Generic longings mingling together tend also to increase indistinctness in the soul. There are mental wants that seem to be stretching out their arms for help, away down at the very bottom of being. There are requests of the mind so far beneath the surface that they only come up to our consciousness with the feeblest echo. It is as if we heard a corpse crying for help out of its coffin after it had been buried. We put our ears to the grave and listen with the closest attention, and think we hear something, but are not sure, and know not whether to dig away the earth or not. There are many desires which, singly, are clear and well-defined; but when they mingle together, their identity is lost. The desire for rest and peace, the constant thirst for happiness and freedom, are quite tangible when alone; but when they run into each other, there is nothing but a vague and general sense of want.

The element of *doubt* should also be noticed. Although the human mind has been trying its power upon a vast variety of subjects for well nigh six thousand years, yet even to-day, with reference to most things, we know nothing certain. Every science has connected with it an unknown or doubtful territory far greater than that which is occupied. All the doubts of the mind by a law of affinity congregate together. A confused mist-land is the result,—a region of gloom, uncertainty, disappointment. In some minds this state of things is painful and utterly overwhelming. John Foster, at one stage of his development, writes thus: "At some moments life, the world, mankind, religion and eternity appear to me like one vast scene of tremendous confusion, stretching before me far away, and closed in shades of the most awful darkness;—a darkness which only the most powerful splendors of Deity can illumine, and which appears as if they never yet had *illumined* it."* Doubt will sometimes go so far as to reject the truth itself. Objections are started without reason. Yet for all this, the element of doubt in human nature is not without profound meaning. It has a basis in finite mind as that stands connected with many of the objects of its investigation. When carried to a certain length, it is perfectly lawful; for it enables one to "prove all things, and hold fast that which is good."

* Life and Correspondence, vol. i, p. 34.

Another reason why a nebulous belt surrounds the soul is the fact that *certain movements of mind cannot be expressed in human language.* There is such a thing as "darkening counsel by words without knowledge." "Mathemetical truth, happily, has formed for itself a language adequate to its purposes; a language real, and which is liable to no ambiguity or variation; but then this is because mathematical science is conversant with the properties of matter and its relations; and therefore the instrument of its conveyance, being homogeneous, is sufficient. But how far otherwise is it when we have to do, either with metaphysical abstractions, or with the heights, and depths, and refinements, of the human passions and affections! On this ground how does it want compass, nicety, power! Language well and truly conveys all those notions that are its own creatures, or that are more modified by it, than they modify the medium of their expression. After having vulgarized and enfeebled our conceptions and our sentiments, language then sufficiently represents and recombines what it has first reduced to its own level. Meanwhile every profoundly impassioned and sensitive mind, and every mind accustomed to hold language in obeyance, during its processes of analysis and abstraction, is painfully conscious of the inferiority of any actual medium of expression that is at its command. In the recesses of the human soul there is a world of thought, which, for the want of determinate and fit symbols, never assumes any fixed form, such as might beneficially constitute a part of the intellectual and moral wealth of the species, or even much augment the wisdom and virtue of the man."*

Ideas of the *future* and the *eternal* have also a degree of dimness surrounding them. The fact that no one knows anything experimentally of a coming existence makes the whole appear like a vast milky-way along which pure spirits may travel, but not men. No curtain is drawn aside for a moment, in order to enable us to gaze upon the eternal habitations of the good and bad. There is a twilight around the soul; and it can do no more than wonder and guess and calculate. From this island-world of the universe where we now are, men are rowed across a dark sea till they reach the continent of eternity; then they take either of two ways as character designates, along which they travel

* Isaac Taylor, "Physical Theory of another Life," chap. viii.

in joy or sorrow, in noon or night, forever. Now and then, fires seem to be lighted up on the mountains of God, by the aid of whose light the shores of eternity are seen, and clouds of visitants waiting to receive the purified. Again we are in the midst of darkness, when gradually a moon looks out from the edge of the horizon, and sending its solitary light athwart the waste of waters, we behold boatmen conveying the lost into eternal exile. This is the way the human mind has acted in by-gone ages. All the strange fancies of men touching the viewless future show plainly enough that there is a portion of the soul in the midst of an eclipse.

As a further explanation of our theme, we may notice the *transcendental* element of the human spirit. Any system of philosophy which attempts to set aside the transcendental is false to the nature of mind. Mere empiricism will never satisfy. It is too cold and tame. It lacks both bottom and top. It may appear simple and reasonable, but it is unreasonable. Such rationalism is irrational. It forgets the supernatural. It lives too exclusively with the finite. All that cannot be measured, weighed, and squared, is put aside.

But man has the faculty of reason, as well as the faculty of understanding; he has *à priori* conceptions, as well as logical deductions. It is true that many of the so-called transcendentalists have with staff in hand walked straight into night and nothing. This has exposed the higher philosophy to ridicule. But yet if we take the trouble, gold can be found as well as dross, wheat as well as chaff. John and Paul were urged forward by transcendental thoughts. Hence their theology has things hard to be understood.

Again, the soul instinctively clings to that which is *mysterious*. A strange pleasure is derived from that which is incomprehensible. The mind is enlivened and educated by mysteries. In certain cases, the obscure affects us more than the clear. The more we know certain objects and persons, the less impression do they make upon us. Too much familiarity hinders powerful emotion. A speaker will sometimes impress strangers, when he fails to impress friends Of course, this is not a universal fact; yet it has meaning none the less. Greater light respecting many things would be no gain to us. Eternity, heaven and hell, as described in the Bible, probably make a more favorable impression on the mind than they would do if more was revealed in regard to them. Where our knowledge fails, *faith* and *humility* are cultivated,—two characteristics of prime importance. It is the mystery of the trinity and the incarnation that feeds and fills Christ-like souls. The idea of the Infinite is sublime in its very darkness. The soul in view of such an august Presence adores and wonders. The Infinite is all around; and the finite like some lonely star is burning dimly in ancient skies. Self is reduced to a mere point; and an ocean of being rolls away in all directions in sublime mystery. As man looks and listens, he can almost imagine that he hears the hallelujahs of God as they die away among the eternal hills like the sound of distant seas.

With these few thoughts upon a very difficult subject, we may see how it is that a dark province exists in the soul. To give an exhaustive explanation of the whole matter is beyond our power. We therefore make no further statements touching the point in hand, but proceed to view it in its relation to the future developments of God.

It must be admitted that the great end of God is the manifestation of himself, and that this manifestation must be *eternally progressive.* It is no less a truth that man is to be a witness of the divine manifestation, and that *he must be eternally progressive* in order to behold the manifestation in all its fulness. With such thoughts relating to man and God, it is clear that great changes will take place in the human soul during the ages everlasting. Under the future ministry of Jehovah, it is supposable that the mind will have power to seize hold of some of the higher principles of philosophy and government, which now are not known; and because not known, confusion and uncertainty are ever about us. Having gained such fundamental principles, it will be comparatively easy to arrive at safe conclusions. The whole intellectual nature will doubtless experience a wonderful revival, and what is now thought out with great difficulty and with astonishing slowness will then be brought to a conclusion with great facility and quickness. Occasionally in the present life we see rare feats of intellectual ability, which suggest what may be expected in the coming life. In men of genius with their intellectual strides, there is found a typology of the future. Under the favcrable circumstances of eternity, the mind may have power to grasp sections and chapters of knowledge at once. Sublime generalizations of truth will be thrown off from the soul, implying the utmost familiarity with multitudes of facts and principles. There will thus be a better understanding of the divine system and Divine Being.

It is not unreasonable to suppose that the bodily orb of vision and the faculty of consciousness will have an equal extension. There is a kingdom of being on the earth so minute that the eye cannot reach it; there is another kingdom beyond the earth of great magnitude, yet because of its distance it cannot be seen; there is only a small realm which can be perceived at one time. May not the celestial body, then, be both microscopic and telsecopic? may it not see the little and the large, the near and the remote, with almost equal precision? The immensity, grandeur, and variety of the divine system, compel us to believe that the individual made to behold this will not be always under that law of limitation which characterizes the present primary stage of existence. Indeed, instead of merely possessing five senses, we may possess five hundred. It is not at all likely that all the properties of matter are now known to us. A change thus so great without, might fitly symbolize the change that will take place within. The circle of consciousness, now so small, may *then* be greatly extended. "Now we see through a glass darkly; then face to face."

Add to this a similar awakening and strengthening of association and memory, and what a vast prospect opens up before the soul! As the laws of association are connected to a great extent with matter, it is possible that the future body may be so constituted that it will send forth perpetual and manifold suggestions to the mind, containing as it were an epitome of the soul's wealth. We know also that memory has a material side, for it is strong in youth and feeble in old age; thus pointing out the probability of great power in the future when once the mind is united to a perfected physical organism. What a vision that will be when suggestion and memory combine together to bring up the darkened past to the light, and when the glance of consciousness shall take in the greater part of the mind's action! It will seem then as if a thousand souls were brought together under the keen gaze of the mental eye, and a thousand knowledges and experiences were dazzling and delighting the one immortal.

It is probable also that man will pass through various transitions in the future state. While character and condition will be fixed—he that is unjust will be unjust still, and he that is holy will be holy still—this does not imply that great changes will not occur during the history of eternity. Even the glorified body may receive new power at the commencement of some remote epoch of heaven,—power needed to meet some new manifestation of God in creation. Inasmuch as the present universe had a beginning, and is necessarily finite, there must be a period however distant when it shall be fully comprehended by the soul; hence it may pass away and give place to a new system, thus calling for a change in the body to fit it for the new materialism that surrounds it. At such transitional moments, there may rise up in the mind powers that have lain dormant ever since the birth of the individual, special use for them not having existed during the whole of the past. There are certainly perfections in the Divine Mind respecting which we have no conception, and there may be perfections in the human mind equally unknown;

yet at some predestined hour of the remotest ages new revelations of God and man may stream forth in perfect unity and fitness. The manifestation of God throughout eternity is to have stages, and each stage is to be higher and brighter than the one that preceded it; so also the soul is to pass through great epochs of perfection, each epoch of perfection preparing the way for the one that is above it.

Hence we infer that the nebulosity of human souls will, in a measure, be dispersed by the light that is to shine along the centuries of eternity. Yet we would have it noted that while much of the present confusion and uncertainty will pass away, this will only be to prepare the soul for the admission of new phenomena that will cloud and puzzle, if not to the same extent as before, yet to a certain extent. Some things that cannot be understood now will be understood hereafter; but, then again, new mysteries will appear in eternity which found no place in time. As the finite can never comprehend the Infinite, there must be heights which no one can scale, and depths which no one can fathom. There will be unsolved problems forever. Faith, hope, and love are three graces that will be needed as long as God lives and the soul lives. Consequently, the truth demands that we say, that there will always be a degree of twilight surrounding the creaturely spirit; yet it will be ever changing in kind and extent as the years of the future roll away. "But the pleasure is, I think, to humble people, in knowing that the journey is endless, the treasure inexhaustible,—watching the cloud still march before them with its summitless pillar, and being sure that, to the end of time and to the length of eternity, the mysteries of its infinity will still open farther and farther, their dimness being the sign and necessary adjunct of their inexhaustibleness." *

* Beauties of Ruskin, p. 426.

CHAPTER II

THE FINITE DISSATISFIED WITH LESS THAN THE INFINITE.

THERE is a tendency in the soul which inclines it to go out to the Infinite. Even though one may not have noticed the drift of his spirit in this direction, and may be unable to state or to comprehend an idea of this kind, yet by a close observation of signs and circumstances he may come to a knowledge of the truth. The sight of lofty mountains whose summits are lost in clouds, of a great sea on whose bosom one sails for weeks with no land in view, of serene and luminous space stretching far away, suggest the idea of the Infinite. The rush and long continuance of terrific storms, the flash of the lightning and beat of the thunder, the sweep of great rivers and water-falls, tend to make one think of the Infinite. The measureless nature of time and the magnitude of the universe convey the same idea. I have even thought that a dark, still. night with the occasional appearance of a star in heaven, along with the feeling of solitude that creeps over the mind at such a time, naturally brings up before the soul the idea of a great Being, against whom none can prevail, and from whom none can hide. When the mind is awed and stilled by some great reality, and its hidden depths touched and set in motion by some great power, there is a manifest tendency then to that which is unbounded. Music also is fitted to awaken profound and inexpressible emotions in the soul. The spirit all intensified thinks and feels about that which is mysterious, divine, and infinite. Music, though it has unwonted power over the minds of men, yet is not a human creation. Its home is not the earth; its native sphere is heaven, where it speaks in the language of eternity to immortal beings. Art and eloquence, too, in their purer manifestations, touch the passions of the soul, and prepare it for a flight to a higher realm. "So surely is it the infinite itself that attracts and charms us, that its highest manifestations do not satisfy us until we have referred them to their immortal source. The heart is insatiable, because it aspires after the infinite. This sentiment, this need of the infinite, is at the foundation of the greatest passions, and the most trifling desires. A sigh of the soul in the presence of the starry heavens, the melancholy attached to the passion of glory, to ambition, to all the great emotions of the soul, express it better without doubt, but they do not express it more than the caprice and mobility of those vulgar loves, wandering from object to object in a perpetual circle of ardent desires, of poignant disquietudes, and mournful disenchantments."*

The reason why the soul is dissatisfied with merely finite objects is because the *image* of the Infinite is stamped upon it. The mind is a godlike creation, and it cannot be at rest without God. The beast is satisfied with what it finds upon the earth, for its nature aspires no higher; but man has that within his breast which links him to the Deity, and so he cannot be contented without him. The soul is made to know and love God, and when it neither knows nor loves him it is unhappy. The faculties may be employed upon nature, but nature without God does not satisfy. The life may be directed with reference to self, but self

* Cousin, "The True, the Beautiful, and the Good," p. 113, Edinburgh ed.

without the All-sufficient is empty. When nature, self, and God are all united there is peace. "God hath suited every creature he hath made with a convenient good to which it tends, and in the obtainment of which it rests and is satisfied. Natural bodies have all their own natural place, whither, if not hindered, they move incessantly till they be in it; and they declare, by resting there, that they are (as I may say) where they would be. Sensitive creatures are carried to seek a sensitive good, as agreeable to their rank in being, and, attaining that, aim no further. Now, in this is the excellency of man, that he is made capable of a communion with his Maker, and, because capable of it, is unsatisfied without it: the soul being cut out (so to speak) to that largeness, cannot be filled with less. Though he is fallen from his right to that good, and from all right desire of it, yet not from a capacity of it, no, nor from a necessity of it, for the answering and filling of his. capacity." "Though the heart once gone from God turns continually further away from him, and moves not towards him till it be renewed, yet, even in that wandering, it retains that natural relation to God, as its centre, that it hath no true rest elsewhere, nor can by any means find it. It is made for him, and is therefore still restless till it meet with him."* The natural image of God in man is eternal; hence the eternal misery of a soul that finds him not. Archbishop Tillotson very beautifully expresses the true idea of the human soul. He says: "God hath wrought the image of himself upon the mind of man, and so woven it into the very frame of his being, that, like Phidias' picture in Minerva's shield, it can never totally be defaced, without the ruin of human nature." Man being thus made, he must be unhappy; his sinful life can bring no peace.

Yet there is a great difference in souls as it regards the feeling of dissatisfaction. Some seem well nigh pleased with what they find about them, and have but a feeble craving for a good that is both divine and infinite. Such look around for a Divinity, much in the same way that children search for treasures they know not the value of. Souls thus darkened and degraded are but so many altars to an unknown God. They are not unlike those whom the Gnostics represent as having only a consciousness of the Archon, not being spiritual enough

* Leighton, Works, i, p. 261.

to have communion with the Supreme. They can think of a World-Ruler, a Power who helps to fill a blank between themselves and the absolute; but to do more than this is impossible. The divine consciousness is so weak and clouded that there are only a few vague strugglings, and a few dim thoughts.

Vestiges of God in the soul of man tend also to explain the fact that the finite is dissatisfied with less than the Infinite. There is the ideal of a perfect law, the ideal of a perfect life, and the ideal of a perfect blessedness for the good hereafter. According to the fulness and finish of these ideals, and according to the distance of our departure from them, will be the torment of the sinning spirit. The fact also that evil is condemned, and the conviction that the wicked should be punished, show that there are both divine principles and divine motions in the human soul. The vilest of men will praise a self-sacrificing spirit, and the most wicked parents will have a desire that their children should be better than themselves. But vestiges of God show themselves the brightest in the souls of the good. Perhaps there is no feeling that has so much of the limitless and the divine about it as the feeling of pure love. The glory of love is that it has no bounds,—it runs out to the Infinite. Whoever, therefore, possesses this sublime feeling cannot but be dissatisfied with that which is merely finite. How natural it is also for the pure mind to make choice of some great truth, to hover about it, and to make efforts to rest in it. The truth is supposed to look like the divine reality; it is either a shadow or a type of it; and so the spirit presses it to its bosom as one does the likeness of a friend who is far away. There are truths which never become old to the good; such as love and redemption, faith and hope, heaven and God. If each of these be analyzed, it will be seen that the limitless element runs through them all. Again, righteous persons may be said to have a taste for the divine. When a godlike action is performed, there is connected with it a peculiar kind of sweetness and pleasure. This pleasure does not spring up in the mind as the result of every action that is performed. The peculiarity, I think, is here—the noble deed that is done is divine; and the pleasure that follows it has a character and a quality from the deed itself, and so that is divine also. He who is merely human knows nothing of divine joy.

One must be a partaker of the divine nature before he can exercise godlike emotion. All that pleasure which saintly men and women have when meditating on divine things and when holding communion with God is plainly of a supernatural character. With such relics of God in the souls of men it is not strange that they should be dissatisfied with whatever is fleeting and limited. In view of the finite they pine away. For a divine good they hunger. Without it they are weary and restless. Echoes of God sound through the soul. Voices cry for the Infinite and the Good.

The tendency to change, so common among men, shows that they are dissatisfied with the temporal and the finite. They are hurried on from object to object, thinking that what is not found in one thing will be found in another. If a treasure has been discovered to-day, the interest awakened by it lasts but for a short period; there is speedily a cry and a craving for some new and different object. A child will be delighted with some new playthings which it has received from a father or a friend; yet at the close of a few days or weeks, it will turn from them with comparative indifference, and will beg for some trifling toy which it sees for the first time in a neighbor's house. Men are but larger children; their valued objects please not always. Dissatisfied are men with all that is limited and imperfect, yet it is next to impossible to drive them away from these; infatuation bids them try again, that perhaps to-morrow will reveal what to-day does not. That some good is found is true, for the finite fits certain parts of the finite; but God is the complement of the soul at all points. The body finds much on the earth; the soul finds very little. Animal men live to a great extent in the *present;* just as the beast has a *now* during which all its wants are satisfied. When man approaches the brute creation he thinks only of the body; and that has no past or future. Spiritual men look to a past which has made them what they are; to a future that may bless them with what they have not. But, whatever the character and standing of human beings, they never find that which most they want so long as they look to the earth and to the perishable about them. They may go here and there, do this and that, as the moments dictate and as circumstances call forth, but there is no rest. There may be a superficial quiet while going somewhere and doing something, but beneath the surface all is uneasy. When man turns his face to the higher worlds and to the Being that is everlasting, he begins to have peace. When the soul has found its centre, and around it ever moves and toward it ever inclines, then it enters into rest.

"It is plain," remarks Bishop Butler, "that there is a capacity in the nature of man, which neither riches, nor honors, nor sensual gratifications, nor anything in this world can perfectly fill up, or satisfy: there is a deeper and more essential want, than any of these things can be the supply of. Yet surely there is a possibility of somewhat, which may fill up all our capacities of happiness; somewhat, in which our souls may find rest; somewhat, which may be to us that satisfactory good we are inquiring after. But it cannot be anything which is valuable only as it tends to some further end. Those therefore who have got this world so much into their hearts, as not to be able to consider happiness as consisting in anything but property and possessions, which are only valuable as the means to somewhat else, cannot have the least glimpse of the subject before us; which is the end, not the means; the thing itself, not somewhat in order to it. But if you can lay aside that general, confused, undeterminate notion of happiness, as consisting in such possessions; and fix in your thoughts, that it really can consist in nothing but in a faculty's having its proper object; you will clearly see, that in the coolest way of consideration, without either the heat of fanciful enthusiasm, or the warmth of real devotion, nothing is more certain, than that an infinite Being may himself be, if he pleases, the supply to all the capacities of our nature."*

The states of mind which are called by such names as *melancholy*, *dejection*, *despondency*, *despair*, point to the fact that the soul is unhinged and not right with God. It is true that the condition of the body may have a tendency to cloud the soul and make it sink down in gloom and heaviness, but the whole working of these states of mind cannot be explained by mere bodily ailments. After due allowance has been made for physical causes, there must yet be something back of them, something spiritual, that will fully account for such mental states. Apart from all materialistic influences, the mind is not satisfied with itself, neither is it generally satisfied with the

* Sermon xiv. "Upon the Love of God."

men and the circumstances that surround it; and so it sinks into an eclipse,—is sad, cheerless, and dejected. The religious element, if it exist at all, is not sufficiently powerful to overcome or to neutralize opposing forces. The tendency of the mind is to doubt. This in fact is the central evil. This isolates the soul; turns away its face from the Deity; makes it droop and turn pale as a plant cut off from the light of the sun. The spirit shut up in darkness has dark thoughts; it broods in solitude; preys upon itself; cannot believe with the totality of the mind,—therefore cannot rest. There is much unhappiness; there is positive misery in the soul; and, what adds to it, hope is like a dying taper. A person thus situated will sometimes destroy himself; and suicide is but the wild symbolism which shows that God is gone and the soul is miserable.

Guilt also may be noted as showing how the finite spirit cannot be satisfied while away from the Divine Being. The relation of man to God has all its significance from the fact that it is a moral relation. The departure from God which takes place when sin is committed is a spiritual departure. Hence the turmoil of conscience when guilt is burning there, points out the great centre and source of mental misery. The very nerve of dissatisfaction is guilt. Indeed, man is oftentimes dissatisfied with that which would otherwise please him, because conscience is angry and condemning. To satisfy a guilty man is by no means an easy matter. Conscience may be stupefied, but not satisfied. Sin is the selection of the finite instead of the Infinite : such a selection never can bring peace to the soul. It is absurd to suppose that God would create man that he might find rest and happiness in the utter rejection of himself. The whole of our mental uneasiness, therefore, springs from the fact of sin in human nature,—sin against the Supreme Being. "It is an oft-repeated fact, that unbelievers in the existence of a personal God, are not able to rid themselves of the warning of that law which God has written in their consciences; and may we not see in this a holy arrangement, by which, when man has entirely sundered the bond of communion with his Maker, another bond should still remain by which it may be possible, by awakening in him the consciousness of inward variance with himself, to bring the wanderer back again to his allegiance."* Doubtless the great schism of

* Müller, Doct. of Sin, vol. i, p. 101.

the soul, by which it feels its misery, may be a powerful instrumentality to lead it back to God, in whom it may find its happiness. In this way natural punishment may be made the auxiliary of supernatural redemption. It would seem to require less divine influence to lead one back to God when he is deeply conscious of guilt and unhappiness than when he is not. But, be this as it may, the terrible fact of remorse sufficiently establishes the topic we are considering. And this is all the more clear when we notice the holy satisfaction of that man whose life is devoted to the service of his Maker. He who is united to God by love has a peace and a joy of which the guilt-stricken spirit knows nothing.

The feeling of *anxiety* is also very suggestive. Whether anxiety be more common than care, I know not. Among the young, neither feeling is experienced to any great extent. Care, solicitude, and anxiety are the heritage of men, —men imperfect and sinful. "These terms express mental pain in different degrees; care less than solicitude, and this less than anxiety. Care consists of thought and feeling; solicitude and anxiety of feeling only. Care respects the past, present, and future: solicitude and anxiety regard the present and future. We are careful about the *means ;* solicitous and anxious about the *end*; we are solicitous to obtain a *good*; we are anxious to avoid an *evil.*"* There must be a kind of twilight about the soul which renders objects somewhat indistinct; so that the mind bends forward with a certain uneasy feeling, not knowing what is beyond it. As the matter is thought over, evil is imagined; it being more natural to imagine evil than good inasmuch as the soul is sinful. Having fastened upon the evil, the mind is pained and perplexed. There is no sure footing; hence the troubled spirit wanders about in a state of anxiety. It can easily be seen from this that man is separated from God; and that not till faith unites the two together and hope illumines the future can there be peace. To a pure mind there can be no real anxiety. There may be a profound sense of responsibility when some great task is assumed; but painful anxiety as to any results is not to be allowed,—that were to betray a spirit of unbelief. The soul of Jesus was greatly agitated was shakng by reason of a great sorrow ; but yet I cannot think that corroding care disturbed his spirit,

* Crabb's English Synonymes, p. 425.

or blighting anxiety withered his heart. The Redeemer was not only sinless, but he was divine; his future therefore was not uncertain; his sufferings and death stood before him as a present reality. It was this fact that struck his soul, and this that threw a loneliness about his being.

Fear is another element of human nature which forcibly illustrates our proposition. This perhaps is the most striking of anything yet mentioned. Fear, although it be not the highest characteristic of mind, is yet, for this very reason, the better fitted to attract attention and to produce conviction. Just witness multitudes in time of a thunder-storm. Completely careless when all is still about them, they tremble when danger is apprehended: by a kind of instinct they flee to God. Simple nature, conscious of its peril, compels a prayer to ascend to the Almighty. The same thing is seen during a storm at sea. Let wild waves break over the vessel—instantly the shrieks of the fearful are heard bearing aloft a prayer to the ear of God. At such a time, there is but one object that man hastens to; that one object is God. See others when dying. They realize that they are about to enter the region of the unknown. A solitude which they never experienced before marks them off by themselves. They are alone in the valley of death. A dire eternity is just at hand, and they fear exceedingly. They remember that God is just. A prayer leaps out of the soul. As the affrighted dog howls instinctively, so man struck with terror cries to God. The sentiment of David is true even here: "What time I am afraid, I will trust in thee."

Now, we do not want a more forcible proof that the finite is dissatisfied with less than the Infinite than we find in the simple working of fear. Why should the soul so quickly and so anxiously go up to the one God? Why to *God?* Let this be answered. It should be carefully noted that the soul is stripped of everything like art when it speaks through fear. Fear is the most elementary expression of human helplessness. The argument from this source is therefore all the more powerful. We see just how the soul acts from the naked stand-point of nature. False opinion nourished by pride may drag the human spirit away from God; but only let fear arise, and in a moment the divine refuge is the one that is thought of. The soul will have God even though it does not want to have him. The constitutional nature, of which God is the author, compels the soul to look upward in spite of the developed nature, of which man is the author. On this account, we often see the same person entirelv different under different circumstances.

Quite an array of testimony might be here introduced from the last hours of sceptics, but we satisfy ourselves with a single reference. "I have always considered the death of Hume as described by Adam Smith, Dr. Black and others, to be a scene of the most flimsy hypocrisy to be found on record. It is obvious that Hume's friends, like those of Voltaire, were anxious that he should evince no sign of misgiving or fear, and should persist in his infidelity to the last. But both he and they over acted so far in the matter, as to betray themselves. They tell us of his great composure; of his utter unconcern as he sat with them at the card-table, knowing himself to be on the brink of the grave; how he could repeat the silly jests which he might have with Charon, the boatman sent according to the fables of Paganism, to carry the dead across the river which was said to divide this world from the world of spirits." "Pitiful gossamer covering of what was going on in the breast of the dying man! Fallen as poor human nature is, she is not so far sunk as this; she is neither so blinded or hardened. She has sympathies that tell of something better, was it merely friend parting with friend, for a period they know not how long, and to encounter they know not what."* The utter unreasonableness of the whole scene and the art manifest in it show that the spirit of the sceptical philosopher was not easy. He needed God more than he was willing to confess. A joke on a death-bed is proof positive that the soul fears the Deity. Men only laugh at death when they would hush the tumult within. Many an unbeliever believes while he does not want to believe. And this makes the proof all the stronger for our important theme. It shows that no specious opinions can avail to cheat the soul out of its God when the great sifting moment comes.

Man trying to live without God is like the ivy without any support to which it may cling. Tall and slender it grows; the rough winds blow it to and fro; it is laid prostrate in the dust. Only let its tendrils fasten upon some tree, and it will entwine itself gracefully around

* Dr. Mathews, "Bible and Men of Learning," p. 178.

it, growing higher and higher. Then though the fierce tempests beat against it, it bends not over; for it has an abiding support. Let the frail spirit of man in the same way find the great God, and all is well. Let the soul cling to Jehovah, entwining itself sacredly around him, going higher and higher forever, and all is complete; for the two were never designed to be apart, but to be together throughout eternity.

CHAPTER III.

THE SOUL A PRAYER WHOSE ANSWER IS GOD.

MAN cannot be understood without God. Possibly God cannot be understood without man. The two natures may point to each other. It is certain, at any rate, that the soul articulates a language which shows a divine origin. That the language is not full and finished, we admit. There are many breaks in it; and without close attention it cannot be understood.

When God made the soul he made it to turn instinctively toward himself. Hence all created spirits are so many distinct prayers, and God is their answer. The fact of sin does not destroy this native movement of the soul. The atheist and the demon have divine requests. He who derides prayer, because of its supposed opposition to the plan of an unchangeable God, prays in his deepest soul to the same unchangeable Being. There is a native necessity about such prayer; it may be called constitutional.

The will may modify it somewhat, but never can render it an impossible characteristic of the soul. Of course, there is no holy yearning of heart; no religious craving for God. It should be understood also that the thirst of the soul is not so definite as the thirst of the body. It shows itself in an indirect way; as when one has a feeling of *uneasiness*. This uneasy state makes man try ten thousand things in order to furnish satisfaction. It also manifests itself in that expressive phrase—*a sense of want*. The soul looks about for that which will fill it. Nothing is found. God alone can meet the craving within. There is another feeling—*the consciousness of vacancy*. All is vain, empty, worthless. Then, again, a man does not know what to do with himself. Everything is wrong; nothing pleases; he is sick at heart. These explain the thought that the soul is a prayer. Frequently the restless spirit is like a man in the water half-dead trying to swim, putting forth efforts unconsciously, aiming to reach somewhat, with a dim sense of wanting to live, and an instinctive movement in that direction. There are mental forces and feelings, tastes and tendencies, which often pass unobserved, and thus count nothing; while to the attentive mind, marking their appearance and comprehending their import, they count a great deal.

Who does not see, for instance, that the sense of *insecurity and change* is an intimation that the soul needs an all-sufficient God? I no sooner begin to think of my nature and condition than I begin to realize my weakness. I see all around me beings like myself, filling a space, occupying a time, then vanishing away; and as I keep gazing on this ever-shifting panorama of mortals, the feeling is deepened that the whole of mankind are in the hand of some unseen Agent, who is acting with a power all his own, and which power he manifests or conceals as to him seems best. The more exact and truthful my contemplations become, the more painful is my sense of insecurity. I am compelled to look around for some stable foundation. The idea of cause also is never truly satisfied till the First Cause is reached. The mechanism and motion of the universe are traced to a Supreme Maker and Mover. In fact, a final cause is as necessary as a first. The mind is restless till it finds the chief reason.

Fate, with all its darkness and fixedness, shows that men reach out to find the Eternal. What a powerful influence has the idea of destiny had upon the development of nations and men! Great characters have generally been inspired by it. They felt that they had a specific work to do, a goal to reach, a prize to win; and so they pressed forward. Then the conceptions of an eternal plan and an infinite Providence have steadied the mind. Sovereignty has generated submission, and submission, peace. A sense of nothingness has ended in finding him who is all and in all. Hope has arisen, which like a divine star has conducted the spirit to its God.

The whole realm of being is but a descending scale from the Absolute One; and all parts look upward. Each department of being is standing as it were on tip-toe, endeavoring to reach that which is above it. Each order is typical. The lower is a prophecy of the higher, and the higher is a prophecy of the highest. The whole kingdom of creaturely existence is but one great prayer ever ascending to God. Sin, of course, has broken up the harmony of the prayer; but yet with all its discords and deficiencies it still goes up to the Supreme. "All lower natures," says Coleridge, "find their highest good in semblances and seekings of that which is higher and better. All things strive to ascend, and ascend in their striving. And shall man alone stoop? Shall his pursuits and desires, the reflections of his inward life, be like the reflected image of a tree on the edge of a pool, that grows downward, and seeks a mock heaven in the unstable element beneath it, in neighborhood with the slim water-weeds and oozy bottom-grass that are yet better than itself and more noble, in as far as substances that appear as shadows are preferable to shadows mistaken for substance? No! it must be a higher good to make you happy."* God loved with all the heart would make the prayer complete. Still, though love be not universal, the native speech of all souls shall ever be—"Our Father which art in heaven."

Indeed, wherever I behold the movements of men, I can see hints and manifestations of a substrate feeling that points to God. It really matters not what may be the object of pursuit or what the course of life, there is everywhere and in everything a symptom which intimates that God is needed. In all the excitements and rush of business which so characterize the present, I am compelled to believe that souls in their deeper nature have

* Works, vol. i. p. 181.

a hungering for the divine; and that the busy speculations, the eager industries, are only indirect and abnormal methods of revealing this strange fact. Unconscious though men oftentimes are of any drift of the spirit towards God, yet the active or indolent life, the restless days and nights, proclaim that an impulse of a lofty kind moves the soul as the breath ot God the spheres; and that even the external and surface workings, though dark and undivine, yet, when viewed as manifestations of an immortal being, they suggest something higher than what could literally be inferred from them. Gambling, for instance, though it may seem to speak simply of amusement or the prize, does more; it shows quite distinctly that here are beings uneasy, because the good for which they were made has not yet been found. The appetite for wealth, which keeps pace with the march of civilization, and which makes men willing to encounter any difficulty to satisfy it, is but the rough herald of a purer appetite, which never can be satisfied with anything short of the Supreme Good. If men did not want God, they would not so eagerly want money. The very greed of covetousness only shows how pressed the soul is without God.

There is a famine within, and a painful, gnawing hunger; and so men wildly seize hold of anything that will seem to satisfy. The miser perishing in the midst of plenty, is but the symbol of a godless spirit starving to death while surrounded by divine treasures.

"God has so inwoven, in the inmost texture of our nature, the title and testimonies of the immortal state for which he made us, that, mingled with the perishable elements of earth, it is, even now, forever around us; it rises in all our dreams, it colors all our thoughts, it haunts us with longings we cannot repel; in our very *vices* it reveals itself, for they cannot charm us till they have more or less counterfeited it." "Our miseries are still the sublime discontent of a being too mighty for the perishable world he dwells in; a deathless spirit is impatient for its native eternity. Yes, the heir of immortality is far from the Father's bosom, by what mysterious doom it skills not to say; suffice it, he awakes to breathe a hostile air, he is born in the enemy's country, and amid the camp of the prince of darkness." "There are aspirations turned astray, that, even in their distortion, attest their origin and purpose. There are warped, and crippled, and polluted hopes, that, even from their dungeon of flesh, still cry for heaven. There are desires that, cursed with the frenzy of sin, run mad through the thronged and heated highways of the world,—yea, that are evolved in all the hideous forms of vice, and intemperance, and blood. But vice itself is not objectless; this insanity is superinduced upon sound faculties; these fires are the fires of conflagration and ruin, but they do not less than others *point to the skies*."*

Why is there such a perpetual struggle for office and honor? Is it not clear that men have fallen from a noble height, and that the strife to reach an earthly elevation but shows the wayward course of mind as its needs and miseries hurry it along. Even pride, that great generic sin which begins the soonest and dies the latest, has somewhat of the golden dust of heaven's pavement clinging to it. Pride tells prophetically of a past when God was all, and man walked with him in peace. It now shows an eyeless, wingless spirit centering its aims on self, while yet there is a latent inkling for the eternal light and the worlds beyond. How much of divine as well

* Prof. Butler, Sermons, vol. i, p. 283.

as human meaning there is in the perpetual discontent of mortals! The soul never balanced and quieted; never free from a depraved nature; never, for once, beholding perfection. Then the feeling of envy: how suggestive that is! The soul wounded, because defeated; wounding others, because they are successful. This intimates that the human spirit was originally designed for a higher world, and for a higher place than is found here. The monarch's son who has wandered from home and from virtue is enraged when his companions are honored, and he is not. Few things so vex the soul as contrasts; and the greater these are, the greater the uneasiness. Give man a dead level, and he would be quiet. But this is impossible. The eternal and the infinite cannot be struck out of his nature. Thoughts of the divine have no death.

How numerous the victims of impatience, fretfulness, jealousy! How much of self-will and wounded pride! These point downward, and upward too. Even in malice, revenge, and dark misanthropy, one beholds a shattered soul wildly proclaiming the need of a God. Deliberate falsehood, plans laid to defraud, preparatory measures to kill, teach the same lesson. Then, too, the strange feeling of self-contempt, how full of significance that is! Not merely does the soul condemn itself, but it despises itself. How could this be possible, unless there was an inward divine tendency? Being sick of self, sometimes ends with a feeling of contempt for the whole surrounding population. All is wrong; life is a burden; death is a terror. With such experiences, the troubled mind, as in sleep, turns itself over towards God; praying without knowing it, praying as in a dream. Rays from the fountain of eternity glimmer in the soul, pointing to an ultimate way never yet followed, never yet loved. Living thus, man frequently makes haste to lose himself in the companies and amusements of time. Speedily he becomes conscious again of wishes and wants, of sighs and miseries,—of eternal thirst and restlessness: the first, which nothing quenches; the second, nothing quiets. On a larger scale, we have riots and wars, thousands wounded and slain; as if the thirst of men and nations could only be quenched with blood. Indeed, I cannot but think that the whole working of sin is but a fearful picture of beings wanting God at the very moment they are striving to live without him.

Besides, whatever men may do there is a

sense of weariness. Even the good have this. I do not refer, of course, to any weariness of body, but to a weariness of soul; as if one's spirit felt that it had been battling with evil during the whole of its existence, that it was struck many a time with sharp cutting blows, and that now it is tired, and longs for a day of deliverance, a sabbath of rest. The present scene of being is so hemmed around with difficulty and discouragement, there is such a downward tendency in souls, making it so hard to lift them up, that the man who has any good in him sighs amidst the ruins of time, and pants for a world where all is right, and for a God who shall meet the most pressing wants of the soul. All those feelings that we usually express by such words as languor, listlessness, insipidity, disgust, are full of meaning. Then, also, the feeling of loneliness, a hidden sorrow, a burden upon the heart, a reaching forth for that which will satisfy,—are but different parts of the shadow of a stray spirit that is feeling blindly around for God. Living in a strange land, man is not well. "The soul is always bursting its limits. It thirsts continually for wider knowledge. It rushes forward to untried happiness. It has deep wants, which nothing limited can appease. Its true element and end is an unbounded good."* Even if we simply find pleasure in that which resembles the Deity, that fact is expressive of tendency towards him. Those who would know nature without knowing God are constrained to love *truth;* and not only this, the very *excitement* that impels them to seek for it is a witness for him who is *the* Truth.

So, too, when I see men aiming to live a moral life; aiming to be merciful as well as just; making efforts to bless the poor, the drunkard, the prisoner, the freedman,—it is very certain that while thus acting the troubled mind finds a degree of rest. All the self-denial put forth to overcome some vicious habit, or to benefit near or distant people, has pleasure connected with it; and partly satisfies the ideal of the mind. The feeling of shame when one is detected in wrong; of remorse at the close of sin; of faith in the immutability of the right; of confidence in the ultimate success of the true and the good,—suggests the idea of a Godward drift of the soul. Why is it that men are so anxious to stand right in the eye of the divine law? Why the various inventions

* Dr. Channing, Works, vol. iii, p. 238.

of guilt to pacify the Divine Being? Why the universal worship of the race, and the great universal prayer? The essential answer is that which constitutes the theme of the present chapter.

As bearing upon our subject, we have another thought. How is it that in all the church centuries Christianity, as a system, has been upheld by *unconverted* men? Religion has been defended by argument when it was assailed, and the church supported by money when it was in want. Men of no piety have attended upon Christian ordinances. The most pungent application of truth they have approved; and, although they felt condemned, they would not venture to condemn the utterances that harmonize with the will of God. It would seem almost as if, at times, the more clearly their sins were revealed, the better were they pleased; and when guilt was allowed no shelter and wickedness no excuse, their satisfaction at such a moment was well nigh complete. I do not know but that with such allies, we might have a Christianity without Christians, a church without members,—unregenerate warriors standing around the temple of God as a wall of defence; while, within, the light of heaven does not shine and the saint of God does not worship; the formal priest alone is at the altar and the word of life before him, but heaven is shut. This current of unsanctified mind is strange; to catch its philosophy is not easy. But does it not seem as if the fugitive spirit had certain broken fastenings of the divine to which it must cling, and that even in its wanderings it has a degree of comfort from the thought that there is a guide-post that points to the kingdom of life, and that it was placed where it is by the Creator himself? Do not unchristian men uphold Christianity because it rests upon the divine, and because they feel that without that they are lost? And yet they may be lost any way; for the peculiarity of the feeling is, that the divine is both received and rejected. Men will stand with awe before the shadow of God, but God they will not love. His worship they will attend, but his name they will not adore. They want God, and yet they do not want him. Perhaps the antagonism here makes the evidence all the stronger, for the fact that the divine can live in the midst of conflict shows that it has a substantial grounding in human nature. Considering the tremendous power of a sinful heart, how tenacious of life must the prayer for God be! No fire of depravity can consume it, and no poison of evil ever put it to death.

But our topic is only fully realized in the soul of the *good.* The inner life of the Christian is a prayer. The shrinking from sin, the desire to be holy, the endeavor to glorify God, convey that thought. Love is prayer. Being born of God, the soul positively and sacredly has a divine tendency. The longing of Christlike souls is altogether different from that of the mere child of nature. It is not only different in degree, but in *kind.* No natural man could say, "As the hart panteth after the water brooks, so panteth my soul after thee, O God." The saved man of heaven is the model of our subject. The purified and perfected soul will be an eternal prayer, finding its constant answer in the eternal God. All the constitutional wants shall be consecrated, directed, and made to centre upon their infinite Object.

CHAPTER IV.

GOD THE HOME OF THE SOUL.

WE began this treatise with God descending to man: we close it with man ascending to God. The word home, which we connect with the last chapter, seems appropriate. It is the end and culmination of mind,—the upshot of the soul is God. There is danger of contemplating home from a merely human point of view. It is the most interesting centre of our earthly life. Our tenderest feelings cluster around it. Joy and grief are awakened in the soul by its continued or sundered companionships. There is a peculiar pleasure in the words—"I am going home." More especially is this true of him who has mingled for years with a remote and strange people, but who now turns his face to the scenes of his childhood. Some of the occupants of his early abode he may not find, yet the place is full of hallowed associations. Even the grave-yard where the departed sleep is consecrated. Both the beginning and the end of life speak of home. There is danger, therefore, that the specific earthly meaning of the word may blind us. It is well to guard against this. When we speak of the home of a soul, the idea seems strange; yet it is really the true idea. The home on earth is but a type of that which is above and beyond it. Its design is to school the fallen spirit, that with lofty intuition it may seek an eternal home with God. In fact, there is but one home, and that is enduring, divine, self-satisfying. One may have his well-arranged house, his pleasant grounds surrounding it, his little family within it; but yet he is not at rest,—the *soul* has not found its home. The most perfect home of man is but a shadow. It almost seems as if the whole family of mankind had been striving to give us glimpses of of a home that is divine. The Egyptians had the idea of *life;* the Persians, *light;* the Greeks, *beauty;* the Romans, *law;* the Jews, *purity;* the Christians, *love.* Perhaps if we could see the whole development of the race completed, we might behold a glorious picture of the ultimate home standing out as the result of this development.

At any rate, no one can help noting the fact

that the idea of a divine home has been generally present to the mind of the species. Even the fancy of transmigration is gilded with the glory of the higher light; for the spirit after many changes may at last reach the communion of the gods. The mystics of all religions have loved to think of themselves as rays of the infinite sun; streams flowing onward to the primal ocean; mysterious waves which sweep the bosom of an eternal sea. Many could say—

> "God is the universal sea of being!
> All beings, e'en the countless hosts of heaven,
> Move towards him as the streamlets to the ocean.
> Is the great sea of Deity in tempest?
> Then all his streamlets toss with agitation.
> Will he, the Parent-deep, dry up those waters?
> He casts them from him to the shore's dry heights.
> Or, will he merge them in his own abysses?
> Then must they yield as stubble to the burning."

Even the atheist and secularist, in their eagerness to banish eternal and divine conceptions from the minds of men, show by their incessant efforts that it is not an easy thing to destroy the aspirations of the God-made soul. They seem like youth, who, since they left their father's house, have lived an abandoned life; and so, not being able to return with any comfort to themselves, deny all connection with the family. The very denial points to the truth.

The Platonic idea that knowledge is *reminiscence* seems to find a realization in our subject; for the mind has an indistinct conception of a home in the *past* from which it has strayed. It seems to be struggling to recollect the totality of the divine idea. There is a vague glory surrounding some ancient beyond, out of which the soul imagines that it dropped; as if a prodigal prince half remembered that he fell from his father's palace window while an infant, never having seen his home since that time. This strange thought of the mind is much the same as a dream which one partially remembers when awake. A certain impression has been left upon the soul, yet the full and true intent of it cannot be gained. How this notion has found a place in the soul of man, it is difficult to tell. Probably it may be a vestige of a primeval truth which remained with the spirit after it sinned, designed evermore to establish the fact of an original fall from God. Most men know that the present state of things is abnormal in its character; and, consequently, it suggests the existence of antecedent development regulated by eternal law. This idea of a past glory darkly divine is almost the common property of the race. The theologies and mythologies of the elder nations all look back. "Though the child longs to pass the hills or seas which inclose his narrow home, yet, when his eager steps have borne him beyond those limits, he pines, like the plant, for his native soil; and it is by this touching and beautiful attribute of man—this longing for that which is unknown, and this fond remembrance of that which is lost—that he is spared from an exclusive attachment to the present."*

How natural it is also for the mind to look *forward* to a good that is to be obtained. Since man conceives that he has fallen from a divine height, and that now he is confined as it were in a prison, he expectantly looks to the future for freedom and blessedness. The man of business intends to retire to the scenes of private life when a sufficiency of money has been accumulated, that thus he may spend the evening of his years in quiet and contentment. The scholar is cheered by his future of fame, and the official aspirant by his post of honor. Why have so many entered convents? A good

* Humboldt, "Cosmos," vol. i, p. 359.

which they craved was thought to be there. Why have theorists and philanthropists pictured out a great day of peace and happiness to the nations? The same yearning for good to come is the answer. The Republic of Plato and the finest works of the imagination are but the outgrowth of this ideal of souls. Even the church of God during its afflictive periods has sent forth the sublimest poetry and prophecy respecting a millennium of rest and peace in the ages to come. The whole world seems to be in a state of pain, and is sighing for a state of deliverance. "The earnest expectation of the creature waiteth for the manifestation of the sons of God." "There is a sort of vague undefinable impression, we think, upon all spirits, of some great evolution of the present system under which we live—some looking toward, as well as longing after, immortality—some mysterious but yet powerful sense within every heart, of the present as a state of confinement and thraldom; and that yet a day of light and largeness and liberty is coming." "The vision of a golden age at some remote period of antiquity, is not unaccompanied with the vision of a yet splendid and general revival of all things."* We cannot but think that

* Chalmers, Lectures on Romans, p. 282.

these anticipations show that the creaturely spirit has some conception of a home with God. The whole of this action of mind with reference to some unknown and future good is the prophecy of perfected blessedness at the right hand of the Supreme. "There is an object for whom we are made, and out of whom we cannot rest,—who is the secret want of our hearts even when we go astray from him; and whom we desire when we know it not."

As the mind also contemplates the great truths of the higher philosophy it seems to move towards the divine goal of being. The sublime speculations of metaphysics and theology carry the soul into a region that is pure, elevating, godlike. Especially is this the case if the objects of thought are eternal and immutable. And, what is instructive, there is a feeling of *peace* and *pleasure* to the well-disciplined mind while engaged on topics and truths that are unchangeable in their nature. The soul rests in the absolute idea, and is happy because it rests. What a relief and a relish come to the created spirit when it grasps the idea of a Cause that is both efficient and final; and what power there is in the idea of law. As we enter the moral sphere, the mind is composed by the conception that right is immutable. The entire philosophy of the reason, as contradistinguished from that of the understanding, brings peace. Hence all finer natures have loved to commune with ideal being. One in this way comes nearer to the fountain-head of all truth—to God. "There is good room to ask whether the peculiar energy of what might be called the mathematical soul does not carry with it a deep meaning, and declare the truth of man's destination at the first, and of his destiny still to take a place and to act a part in a world of manifested truth and of eternal order. Do we venture too far in saying that, when mathematical abstractions of the higher sort take possession of a vigorous reason, there is placed before us a tacit recognition (one among several, all carrying the same meaning) of the fact that the human mind is so framed as to find its home nowhere but in a sphere within which the absolute and the unchangeable shall stand revealed in the view of the finite intelligence?"* The quiet that settles down upon the soul during such moments of abstraction is proof that it was made to find its blessedness in the bosom of change-

* Isaac Taylor, "World of Mind," p. 165.

less Love. It is pleasant to see even in man fallen vestiges of his former greatness; and pleasant to hear prophetic annunciations of a land of peace and light that lies far away beyond the abodes of time and mere sensible reality. There is something exceedingly attractive in the very height to which the soul can carry itself, and in the very pureness of the eternal sky where nothing sparkles and shines but the supernatural. It certainly is a fact that the soul is nearer its own native region while thus situated; for it is far above the strife of human tongues and the noisy tumult of earth,—away up in the realm of the supersensible and the divine, where certainty reigns forevermore, and absolute necessary truth conducts the mind to the very presence of the Everlasting.

If I am not mistaken, man goes through life with a sense of *uncompleted being*. There is always something wanting. A beginning is made, but a wholeness never results from this. There is nothing like totality or rounded completion. This makes man uneasy and dissatisfied. He never finds what his nature demands. There is something even in the holiest minds upon earth which intimates that the life here and the experience here are but half finished. With this state of human nature, there is an ideal in the mind which points to the *future* as a place of *completed being.* It is not at all necessary that there should be clear and distinct conceptions with respect to this perfected condition. Even the best of men are unable to understand the fulness of blessedness that will constitute the heritage of a saved soul. It is enough to have the simple conviction that the whole being will be satisfied. Now, we cannot help thinking that this movement of mind is really another step towards the divine home of spirits. The sinful soul perceives that perfected and finished life is hereafter. All men have a heaven which is to be the consummation of good. We may even say that the race has had four great visions of blessedness: The first, respecting a primitive state of purity and happiness. The second, when there was a general expectation that some great personage would appear,—pointing to "Christ the desire of all nations:" The third, foretelling a day of prosperity and peace to the future people of earth. The fourth, finding its realization in the eternal state. The great terminal period with man individually and collectively is not in time, but in eternity. There seems to be a current in the sea of the soul that has a specific direction of its own. The mind unconsciously turns to one point. It seems to be attracted towards some great object hidden in the distance, even as the stellar hosts incline towards a central universe. The thought of completed being is dimly associated with God. Man was not made to be happy in himself; neither was he made to find completion in a place, as heaven; but in a person, and that person Divine. It is an ultimate truth that when any being attains the end for which it was created it finds rest. Man feels that he has not reached the end of his creation, for he is unhappy; and, consequently, he imagines that absolute rest will in some way come to the soul when it is carried along by the infinite love and plan of God. Says John Owen: "Our love unto God ariseth from a sense of our own wants—our insufficiency to come unto rest in ourselves, or to attain unto blessedness by our own endeavors. In this state, seeing all in God, and expecting all from the suitableness of his excellencies unto our rest and satisfaction, our souls cleave unto him, with a desire of the nearest union whereof our natures are capable.

We are made for him, and cannot rest until we come unto him."*

Here we notice now that suggestive fact of our nature, viz., the demand for *unity*. The common working of the intellectual powers is guided by this natural tendency or law of our being. In the sphere of our moral life, there is a constant agitation and fluctuation of soul because this fixed unity is not found. There is a rasping unhappiness very frequently when one cannot see that anything has been done which is sinful in itself. Yea, at the very moment when there is a good degree of joy on account of some benevolent act or feeling, there is also back of this a secret dissatisfaction. This is the soul crying out in its own native dialect for oneness. The sense of *pain*, which really never forsakes the spirit of man in the present life, is the witness of disunion. The mind possessing this experience feels that the whole nature should be in a state of oneness with itself and with God. The principle of unity will not allow the soul to rest out of the final Object. The culmination of all good is realized when the great unitary law of existence connects the finite with the Infinite. It

* Works, vol. i, p. 153.

seems probable that the union of the persons in the Godhead is the sublime ideal of that oneness which ought to characterize the entire commonwealth of mind. The trinity in unity is doubtless the archetype which God is aiming to realize throughout boundless space and endless time. Hence the significant prayer of Christ, "That they all may be one; as thou, Father, art in me, and I in thee." President Edwards, in his "Dissertation concerning the end for which God created the world," makes use of the following language: "God's respect to the creature's good, and his respect to himself, is not a divided respect; but both are united in one, as the happiness of the creature aimed at, is happiness in union with himself. The creature is no further happy with this happiness which God makes his ultimate end, than he becomes one with God. The more happiness the greater the union: when the happiness is perfect, the union is perfect. And as the happiness will be increasing to eternity, the union will become more and more strict and perfect; nearer and more like to that between God the Father, and the Son; who are so united, that their interest is perfectly one. If the happipiness of the creature be considered as it will be, in the whole of the creature's eternal duration, with all the infinity of its progress, and infinite increase of nearness and union to God; in this view the creature must be looked upon as united to God in an infinite strictness."* This high and ultimate conception of unity does not rest satisfied with making God the home of the soul, but rather the home of *all spiritual orders.* Even fallen spirits in their eternal wanderings will ever have before them the vision of a lost home,—a vision which will intensify the pain of inward disunion, and render terrible the sense of uncompleted being. As sailors while crossing the Caribbean Sea imagine that they hear the sound of bells of sunken islands, so outcast spirits will fail never to hear the echoes of a lost heaven and a lost God. "O my God, how happy is the soul who finds his delight in thee, since he may abandon himself to thy love, not only without scruple, but with commendation. How firm and lasting is his happiness, since his hope cannot be disappointed, because thou wilt never be destroyed, and neither life nor death shall separate him from the object of his desires; and that the same moment which overwhelms the wicked

* Works, vol. ii, p. 256.

and their idols in one common ruin shall unite the just with thee in one common glory; and that as the one shall perish with the perishable objects to which they were attached, the others shall exist eternally in the eternal and self-existent Object to which they are so strictly united."*

From the standing ground that we have now reached, we can see that a divine home for the creaturely spirit is inseparably connected with two ultimate mental states; viz., *rest* and *blessedness*. There are no words that fall so kindly and softly on the troubled soul of man as these two. When I search for the ultimate demand of souls in ruin that ultimate demand is rest. And this, too, is clear, that no mere outward quiet will answer. It is not that of place and circumstance; not material and bodily; but it is wholly spiritual. It is the soul that needs the rest, and must have it. I care not what may be the external condition; it may be as serene, beautiful, peaceful, as heaven itself; and yet, if the soul is not harmonized, all is but a pleasant mockery, and the evil is only increased by the mighty contrast. The collective wicked of earth may be transported to

* Pascal, "Thoughts," p. 376.

the peaceful regions of the saved, yet they would groan with agony; for it is the soul that is conscious of inner misery, and that pants for repose. It must be observed that rest and blessedness are *results*. We must consequently find that which will produce these states. Home then will be reached.

Our first statement is, that rest and blessedness are the result of *perfect order* in the soul. There is a great law or principle in the human mind which points to a region of perfect order as that which alone is desirable. This ideal of order makes one ever dissatisfied with confusion. A splendid edifice, all the parts of which are well proportioned, invites one to look, and to continue looking, with manifest delight. A garden all arranged in symmetry compels the eye to gaze upon it with satisfaction. If listening to a company of singers all of whom unite to produce one piece of music in perfect harmony, you are delighted, and wish the whole to continue on account of the evident satisfaction which it brings to the soul; while again, if there be nothing but a scene of discords, this grates upon the ear, and you wish the whole performance to cease. When the entire mind acts according to the design of God, it is enraptured and at rest at the same time. Imagine only one sin to exist, and unrest would follow. The ongoing of the soul would then be like the eye with a burning spark in it; it is inflamed, and weeps with pain, and has no rest till the spark is removed. Suppose that a hair in some way has connected itself with the mainspring of a watch; the whole movement is one of evident uneasiness; and, if the watch could speak, it would say that it was restless and unhappy. Remove the hair, and the working would all be natural and according to the design of the maker. Even so is it with the soul that is freed from all error and moral corruption. Every part fits and harmonizes; and as there is nothing to create a jarring, a sweet peace spreads over the entire mind and a divine joy animates the whole being. What if the whole realm of mind were in unison with itself and in unison with the Eternal Spirit! How unspeakably blessed such harmony of existence! The very conception of universal and eternal order diffuses a quiet happiness over the soul; even as the dreams of dying saints paint the countenance with joy, and cause a smile of gladness to linger there after the spirit has ascended to the communions of God. The perfect and divine home of souls is certainly reached when perfect order is thus realized.

Again, rest and blessedness are the result of *perfect activity*. The idea of rest is very frequently associated with the idea of inactivity. It would seem that the thought is taken from the outward and material sphere in which men are accustomed to move in the present life. When one is weary with labor, rest and non-labor connect themselves together. Cessation from toil brings rest to the body. Hence, too, of the rest in sleep, when there is both inactivity and unconsciousness. But this is purely materialistic, and wholly unlike that mental quiet and satisfaction which follows perfect activity. In bodies that are sound and healthy, a sensation of rest and pleasure results from well-directed exercise, which bears some resemblance to the mental states. We suppose also that in the future life the body celestial will be a fit organ for the soul; it will aid the spirit instead of cramping it, because the principle of order just mentioned will characterize the two natures alike; and thus, there being the highest harmony between them, the highest activity may be exercised with safety. It is well known, that the sweetest peace is obtained at the very time when benevolent action and emotion are perpetuated by the affections and will; and if all schismatic and unharmonious elements were removed from the mind, the sabbath blessedness of heaven and of God would be its rich possession forever. I think we may be safe in affirming, that the beatitude of the Divine Being is intimately connected with his activity. We cannot for a moment admit the conception of a passive Deity. Even amidst the vast solitudes of eternity, while as yet the clock-work of creation had not commenced its movements, the Most High was intensely active,—active in the beginningless loves and communions of the three divine persons. The soul that is fashioned after the divine image seems made for eternal activity; finding satisfaction to its whole nature only in this way. Even in sleep, there is good reason to believe that the mind is active; for let one be awakened suddenly, and he finds that he was thinking, he was in the midst of a dream. That we are unconscious of this constant night-thought is no objection. "There are powers in man, the activities of which lie beyond the sphere of consciousness." If we have intense feelings of pleasure and pain during sleep, it is likely that these will be more easily remembered than simple processes of thought; for what we feel is more generally within the circle of consciousness than what we think. Yea, so intent is the mind upon action that there is frequently a struggle to attend to a number of things at one time; as when the extemporaneous speaker thinks not only with reference to present utterance, but also with reference to some future part of the discourse; or, as when the skilled musician reads the notes before him, sings, plays, uses his feet, thinks of what is foreign to the business he is engaged in, apparently at the same instant. From all this, it is clear that activity is the grand constituent of mind; and when perfect, divine peace and pleasure follow from it.

Furthermore, the joy and peace that characterize souls with God spring from a *sense of perfect safety*. Every one knows how much of misery comes to the mind from doubt. The person is made to go from side to side, not knowing what to think or what to do. This of necessity produces much restlessness. The want of certainty agitates and weakens the mind at the same time. Then the element of fear comes in, and that makes the whole being to quiver. Am I sure that my faith is well founded? Many have been self-deceived, and why may not I be also? Thus it can be seen how much of internal discord and unhappiness arise from these different sources. But when one is with God all this is gone. There is no doubt, no fear, no danger of self-deception. There is a most perfect sense of safety, and consequently the entire soul is quiet, is at rest. There is not even the distant supposition of evil. A world of restlessness is produced by that which *may be*, but which never is. The soul with perfect order and activity acts not in this way. And this, too, should be noted, that the saved spirit has not to look away to some future when it expects to be with God, but it *is* with him. Besides, the whole of eternity is one vast scene of safety. Man purified may think of distant ages that are to come and pass onward like the great systems and constellations in the sidereal heavens, but no change in the annals of eternity destroys the sense of safety that fills his soul. And the chief reason now is that man is holy. No scar is seen on any countenance, memorial of ancient crime. A visitor from some distant world would never know that the mighty array of glorified men were once with sin defiled. The eye is clear as the stars of God, and the voice that hymns the eternal anthem is mellow and sweet as the sound of seraphim while they chant the morning psalm of heaven. Whether these saved immortals be upon mountain summit clear, or beneath the shade of the tree of life, whose roots are nourished by the river of God; on the palace walls of glory, or around the great white throne,—all are alike. Each blooms with eternal youth, and each tells the story of a wondrous love; a love warm as the summers of eternity, and soft as the dew that falls upon the hill of Zion.

Indeed, we may say that all good is realized in the divine home of souls. Nothing is wanting. God satisfies the entire nature. There is a totality of blessedness. Man is unhappy no more. "Lord, I have viewed the world over, in which thou hast set me; I have tried how this and that thing will fit my spirit and the design of my creation; and can find nothing in which to rest, for nothing here doth itself rest, but such things as please me for a while, in some degree vanish and flee as shadows from before me. Lo, I come to thee, the eternal Being, the Spring of life, the Centre of rest, the Stay of the creation, the Fulness of all things! I join myself to thee, with thee I will lead my life and spend my days, with whom I am to dwell forever, expecting when my little time is over to be taken up ere long into thy eternity."

THE END.

www.ingramcontent.com/pod-product-compliance
Lightning Source LLC
LaVergne TN
LVHW010141110826
845151LV00002B/398

* 9 7 8 1 4 2 5 5 4 0 1 2 8 *